The Black Toad

Alchemy of Body, Spirit, & Stone

Ron Wyman

Published by
Mandrake of Oxford
PO Box 250
OXFORD
OX1 1AP (UK)

We seek to unveil the world,

and its wilderness.

The serpent of Mercury winds through it.

The toad holds its secret.

See its bright stone in darkness.

This book on spiritual alchemy presents an initiate's undertaking of the internal alchemical process. It is a pathway of vision and illumination; and with particular emphasis placed on the induction of the alchemical dream, this movement becomes a visionary transition and passage. The practitioner's psyche moves through the paths of the *Opus Magnum,* and these paths have a goal—the attainment of the Philosopher's Stone. It is the internal alchemy that acquires access to the ethereal level of the body, and eventually to the enactment of the alchemical Will.

Contents

Alchemical Emblems

Page 23. Michael Maier, Emblem 4, *Symbola aureae mensae*, Frankfurt, 1617.

Page 46. Leonhart Thurneisser zum Thurn, 'Alchymya,' *Quinta essentia*, Steinman, Leipzig, 1574.

Page 49. Michael Maier, Emblem 7, *Atalanta Fugiens*, de Bry, Oppenheim, 1618.

Page 52. Lambsprinck, Emblem 6, *The Book of Lambspring*, Jennis, Frankfurt, 1625.

Page 55. Woodcut 1, *Rosarium philosophorum*, Frankfurt am Main, 1550.

Page 57. Woodcut 2, *Rosarium philosophorum*, Waldkirck, Basle, 1593.

Page 60. Johann Daniel Mylius, 'Putrefaction,' *Philosophia Reformata*, Jennis, Frankfurt, 1622.

Page 62. Basil Valentine, Engraving 12, *Azoth*, Frankfurt, 1613.

Page 64. Lambsprinck, Emblem 3, *The Book of Lambspring*, Jennis, Frankfurt, 1625.

Page 68. Sir George Ripley, *The Ripley Scroll*, printed in David Beuther, Engraving 4, *Universal und Particularia...* Hamburg, 1718.

Page 104. Woodcut 18, *Rosarium philosophorum*, Frankfurt am Main, 1550.

Page 113. *Alchemical and Rosicrucian compendium*, Lower Rhineland (?), ca. 1760.

All other illustrations by the author.

Introduction

Alchemy is revered for many reasons, as it acquired an assortment of branches through its long history. Its developments and changes occurred alongside human history, and it has ancient and uncertain beginnings.

There may be several reasons to take a contemporary interest in alchemy. It steps beyond questionable limits set by the physical sciences, it contains long-established areas of knowledge of medicine, and it elucidates the depths of the human psyche in profound ways. This book is concerned essentially with spiritual alchemy, sometimes called internal alchemy, as transformation of the human psyche.

From the times of its early formations, alchemy's processes have been illustrated through the circle, or the wheel. The cycle is the basis through which the human psyche changes and reforms onto greater levels. Through a cyclical basis of personal transformation alchemy then offers the occultist a well-grounded, powerful, and also enjoyable ascending path to take. It involves, through its phases of the

Opus Magnum, the Great Work, as it is called, a natural, deeply rooted and effective form of metamorphosis.

As spiritual praxis the alchemical process begins by the practitioner's intention to set his or her self onto a pathway. This pathway then includes levels of attainment reached through cycles of the *opus*.

The pathway of spiritual alchemy then involves deep cycles that descend and ascend. This cycling traditionally enters a depth or a darkness, a midnight of constellation, and a formation or renewal at the dawning of each cycle's illumination or realization.

The essential goal of the alchemical cycle is to attain the Philosopher's Stone, the *lapis philosophorum*. This is the essence of the attainments, accomplished through a spiritual and internal alchemy of the Stone, as transformation of the human psyche and body. And all of this takes place within the alchemical vessel, or *vas hermeticum*, as metaphor and representation of the practitioner's soul, or spiritual self, also at times referred to as the daemon.

The alchemical pathway is presented through European alchemy and the Western Hermetic tradition. The archetypal and religious contexts are given mainly through the traditional alchemical deities inherited from pagan Greek culture, and from Judaeo-Christian thought and Kabbalistic theory. There are certainly equivalents, perhaps to every aspect of this pathway, within the Chinese Taoist, the Indian Hindu, and the Arabic and ancient Egyptian alchemical traditions. The European Northern traditions may also be related in many ways, as well as the various Shamanic traditions. These other contexts are referenced at times, but full understandings should be sourced from within those traditions. And this pathway is presented in a schematic way allowing for variance through these other traditions.

The alchemical pathway is a natural path to take. Its levels of attainment are symbolised and adorned with a diversity of natural and earthly imagery, often metaphorised as the climbing of a mountain, as the Mountain of the Adepts. But, this natural aspect of the *opus* is not found simply in its settings and metaphors. It is natural because its pathway, and the entirety of its phases and imagery, are mysteriously inherent in the human psyche, which will appear to the practitioner as the *opus* traverses its paths.

Despite this Western centring of alchemy, it was partly through the work of Carlos Castaneda that I acquired my own abilities. His position within authentic Native American spirituality is uncertain. But, because certain elements of his work have been essential to the experiences and understandings given, he is taken seriously as original knowledge.

Considerable emphasis is placed on dreaming practices. This is brought about through lucid dreaming and through highly objectified and reality enforced dreams, derived partly through methods described by Castaneda. Through these practices, the *opus magnum*, when it is begun, acquires highly vivified and impressive visionary accompaniment.

When alchemy of the human psyche and alchemical dreams are discussed the first area of modern and contemporary thought that comes to mind is C. G. Jung and Jungian psychology. An occult approach, however, is not essentially psychoanalytic. Jung's dream analysis is largely agreed with, but there are essential differences in the approach. Though Jung understands the importance of dreams and imagination in alchemy, he did not involve himself with the development of dream perception in itself. His goal of wholeness, as a process of 'individuation,' symbolised by the mandala, is not a wholeness of the spirit reached through ethereal or 'ectoplasmic' changes within the body and soul, as will be described here; though there are allusions to this kind of wholeness in his works. Another aspect of the alchemy important for an internal alchemy and for Jung is an experience of the human shadow; though the shadow's appearing and transformative natures will differ in an occult approach. And Jung did not have as a goal the development of an occult Will to the extent described here. Jung as psychoanalytic theorist, though he had many occult interests, did not approach alchemy in its original and early sense.

And then dream interpretation will be grounded and centred somewhat differently than in Jungian theory, creating a separate perspective on the alchemical dream process.

The occult path endeavoured through original alchemy is a difficult one. It requires years of work enacted by the adept, and can extend on for a lifetime. It is not an exclusive path, as there are various degrees to which its levels of attainment may be realised; which, even on beginning levels, are certainly not unavailing. Its full realisation, however, is a definite and separate realm of experience that requires devotion and ability.

There are three cycles of the Great Work given here, wherein the thresholds reached by these cycles are each exceptional achievements. And each level of attainment becomes more extraordinary. The cycles are then each individually described through seven phases of the *opus*.

The initial threshold attained involves the enactment of intentional dreaming. Highly objectified, lucid dreaming should be fairly well established in the practitioner prior to entering the pathways of the alchemical vision. The *opus* then acquires its essential grounding as a dream-path, in which the alchemical vision becomes highly realistic and frequent. There have been many prescriptions proposed to accomplish lucid dreams, and there is a set of prescribed acts given here. The level that must be attained is not simply a lucidity however, but involves a strong, physical constitution of the body within dreams. It is a practice, which most persons will master only after surmounting a great obstacle set on their path. But, on a positive note, and as with all of the levels of alchemical attainment, once this threshold has been reached those abilities are permanent.

The second threshold requires that the practitioner gain access to the aethers. This level, attained through the *opus*, requires that the practitioner has fully entered the alchemical dream path. Through this path the Peacock's Egg is realised, and the occultist gradually acquires a state of being that may be understood as evolved, or re-centred. The appearing of the peacock's tail, the *cauda pavonis*, within the alchemical vessel, is traditionally of great significance. It is described then as the peacock's egg, as it unveils the coloured aethers of the ethereal body and aural field. Its details and its methods of mastery are described then in the subsequent work *The Peacock's Egg*. Its threshold of attainment is a coloured luminosity and extraordinary internal alighting and awakening of the Stone. This alighting is accomplished through the practitioner's involvement with the human shadow, as an undergoing of the blackening or putrefaction phase of the *opus*. The second threshold means a purification of the body and its vessel, and that the physical body reverses its own decay and regenerates, as one becomes the alchemical Salamander.

The *magnum opus* is placed within traditions of acquiring a Lesser Stone and a Greater Stone. The second threshold attains the Lesser Stone and the third threshold of attainment involves the formation of the Greater Stone, which may be called the occultist's Will. This is a more extraordinary achievement that certainly requires many years of practice. However, this Will is already present within the first two cycles, without which they could not be reached. And the first two cycles open the pathway to this third threshold.

As far as concerns my own accomplishments, I have attained the first two levels, while descriptions of the third are to some extent derived and based in others' works. Most of the dream imagery and alchemical imagery mentioned in this book I experienced myself while undergoing the Great Work.

R.W.

The Nature of Alchemy

The diversity of methods and practice of the *Opus Magnum* within the long history of alchemy is immense. In view of that history it becomes apparent that there is no single, true understanding of alchemy. What we are given is a vast assortment of works, which have similarities, of processes, materials, ideas, imagery, and archetypes, presented through various pathways and understandings.

It has long been asserted that there is certainly false alchemy. In the Middle Ages false practitioners were called the 'puffers,' because the puffing of the bellows used to increase the heat of the alchemical fire became a central concern, as alchemy degraded into a widespread pursuit for the physical production of gold. They have their own important history, in fact, as chemical discoveries originated there, and they are associated with the break that occurred between alchemy and chemistry. Today, however, our understandings of alchemy are formed mainly through the many manuscripts left to us by the true alchemists, who may have erred in their undertakings, but who remained true to their art. And some assume that we have been given the truths of alchemy through their texts.

The essential ideas that form the alchemical process, having accumulated over time, originated from visionaries, who received their understandings through dreams and personal enlightenment. Alchemy is in fact embedded and hidden in the human psyche, and may be discovered in full in personal solitude, without the assistance of historical texts. Alchemical enlightenment also exists on an open field, which has on its horizon yet undiscovered territory. And then, despite alchemy's vast landscape and complex multiplicity and mystery, the practitioner of the Great Work will, without exception, encounter forms, images, icons, and archetypes that remain essential, and repeat themselves for every alchemist.

The major pathway of alchemy has, from its beginnings, persisted to be the Quest for the Philosopher's Stone. The stone acquired a variety of interpretations and names through its history. Sometimes these refer to the primary matter, or *prima materia*, that it is to originate from, and sometimes to the elixir, jewel, or gold that it becomes in its manifest state.

This book is titled after the alchemical Black Toad. The toad is one of the many symbolic animals visualised in alchemy, and has a long history in occult traditions. The black toad represents, the primary matter involving the black and poisonous nature of the alchemical putrefaction, essential to the *Opus Magnum*. It then has a mythological jewel in its head representing the stone. Because it inhabits underground caverns and tunnels it represents the journey to the Underworld, an essential experience the practitioner undertakes within the *opus*. And in the *Bufo* toad genus the toad's poison is a bufotoxin, also called 'toad's milk,' in some species being psychoactive and hallucinogenic, representing visionary alchemy. The toad is a mysterious image that contains within it many aspects of the *magnum opus*, as it also represents the alchemical vessel itself. It is, on the one hand, an initiate's image, a beginning, a first matter, and an invitation to the Underworld and pathways of visionary alchemy.

The primary matter is that which the practitioner begins with, the original matter that is to be transformed. It is often thought to be a base or crude substance, something common or mundane. And from this matter the stone is formed, which is not necessarily a stone at all. The stone is also generally not to be confused with the alchemical gold. The stone is the heart and tincture of the gold, and is sometimes thought of as a touchstone. It pertains to the golden nature of the stone's level of attainment and realisation. It is a pure or extraordinary gold that was sometimes seen to result from a transmutation of metals, often of a base metal such as lead. For some the stone was thought of as this extraordinary gold, but for most alchemists the philosopher's stone is an unknown element or substance.

Historically the pursuit of the stone may be separated into two areas: internal or spiritual alchemy, as the alchemy of the human spirit, soul, and body, and external or practical alchemy as the quest for an actual physical stone or elixir. The concern for internal alchemy will perceive external alchemy as a secondary representation of spiritual praxis and discipline. External alchemy and its material nature are not thought to be a base or ignoble form of alchemy, but rather objective or symbolic representation of its processes, important for its imagery and devices. The human body and spirit; their hidden chemistry, that includes the dreams, visions, and archetypes of the human psyche, are then referred to at times in terms of the alchemical vessel and its internal workings and processes.

From the earliest times alchemy has had a spiritual basis. This is the case in its Eastern and Western origins, within Chinese and Egyptian alchemy. The emphasis on the material transformation of metals is essentially Medieval in origin. And the extent to which spiritual levels are emphasised through alchemy's history is various and sometimes hidden or obscured, often through the symbolic language used in alchemical texts.

At times the primary matter, the initial, physical substance of the *opus* that is to be transformed, gets confused or conflated with the mercurial essence or aether; the unknown substance intrinsic to the *opus*, and to all of nature. The term *'prima materia'* can refer to either or both of these: the first (primary) substance of the *opus*, or the mercurial essence (primal essence) of the *opus* and of all of nature.

The idea of an infinite substance dates back at least to the Pre-Socratic philosophers, which is not necessarily a substance, per se. The alchemists named Mercury as the essential god of this unknown energy; who is the *Spirit Mercurius*, and also, through the earliest Western history of alchemy, the Egyptian Thoth, and the Greek Hermes. This energy is not air, water, or fire, but is often spoken of in terms of these. And a basic premise of alchemy, extending throughout its history, is that this unknown element, often named the quintessence, is contained in all things.

Jung refers to the 16th century philosopher and alchemistic theorist Paracelsus regarding the *prima materia:*

He says that this unique (*unica*) *materia* is a great secret having nothing in common with the elements. It fills the entire *regio aetherea*, and is the mother of the elements and of all created things.[1]

The *prima materia* is then the essence the *opus:*

The basis of the *opus*, the *prima materia*, is one of the most famous secrets of alchemy. This is hardly surprising, since it represents the unknown substance that carries the projection of the autonomous psychic content.[2]

The transformative process is then often thought to involve a movement toward an essence, wherein a 'higher' nature exist. And so the initial substance of the *opus* already, in some sense, contains the stone, and base metals were thought transmutable into gold because they already contain this gold.

Spiritual alchemy, however, will understand the human body as being, or itself containing, the *prima materia*, which manifests the Stone, the *lapis,* through an internal alighting.

The Body

The primary matter is then simply the human body. It is the body in its initial shadowed state. As such, it is also the body in its crude or base physical state, wherein the attainment of the Stone spiritualises the body, so to speak. This primary matter was sometimes compared to the state of man after the ending of the Golden Age, or after the fall in the Garden of Eden, wherein the acquisition of the stone is then a return to a paradisiacal state.

With Jacob Boehme alchemy in Europe became thoroughly spiritual and independent of practical, laboratory alchemy. Boehme compared this leaden state of the body after the fall to "the gross ore in Saturn, wherein the gold is couched and shut up; his paradisiacal image is in him as if it were not, and it is also not manifest."[3] In Greek myth Saturn was overthrown by his son Jupiter, representing the end of the Golden Age, and was put in the Underworld. Alchemy then attempted a reconnection to Saturn in the Underworld and its gold.

The human body in its crude state is also represented by the toad, and the putrefied black toad.

The toad symbolically dies and putrefies within the alchemical process, as the old body dies. It becomes the discarded body, and the discarded self, which will also manifest in alchemical dreams. The toad dies and decomposes in the *Vision of Sir George Ripley*, or this cold state is found in its underworld hibernation. The toad's death is essential to the Toad Bone ritual, of the becoming of the Toad Witch. It is left near an anthill, its flesh removed by the ants, its skeleton retained by the witch. It represents the Saturnine lead of the alchemical process that will be transmuted, relinquishing the gravity of the shadowed self. In

Michael Maier's *Symbola aureae mensae*, the eagle cannot attain its height as it is chained to the toad.

And, more insightfully, as the toad also re-emerges, it will be seen to represent the bodily shadow and its underworld nature.

The attainment of the stone involves a realisation of the spiritual body. The ethereal body, or astral body, or subtle body acquires various understandings through alchemy's history. It is described by modern alchemist Johannes Helmond:

> This inner, invisible astralbody is sometimes called Proteus; he can assume all the colours, forms and shapes of the world. He is the Corpus sideribus of Paracelsus, sometimes called Evestrum or Mumia, the microcosmic Magnet (Magnes microcosmi), because he is the life-maintaining, indestructible and attracting Principle in the Human Being.[4]

Various attributes are assigned to it; it is protean, magnetic, and indestructible. Life is defined by Paracelsus as a "certain embalsamed Mumia, which preserves the mortal body." The body lives from the Mumia;[5] which refers to the substance used to embalm 'mummies.'

The subtle body also has a place within Kabbalistic theory. It belongs to the doctrine of the *tselem*, the astral body, also related to the *tsel*, the shadow. The "shadow is the external projection of the inner *tselem*,"[6] notes Gershom Scholem. The shadow is seen to have a hidden nature that reflects a hidden Other.

The occult shadow and the human shadow are comparable, or parallel, to the two Mercuries often discussed in alchemy. Boehme describes them as the 'divine Mercury' who changes the 'wrathful, poisonous Mercury' into pure gold.[7]

The Greek Underworld was also thought of as a shadow kingdom, and place of death, through which one is reborn. It is also associated with an invisibility, *a-eidês*, the non-visible, or Hades, and has early associations with chthonic occultism.

The *magnum opus* becomes then a type of light and shadow transformation, as a new light and shadow are born, attaining the spiritual body.

Much of our Western understandings originate from the Greeks. And since our concern is with internal alchemy some history of definitions are given. It is likely that the subtle body, or something similar, had early Greek understandings as the *daimôn*, or daemon. Then in later Greek and Western thought three other distinctions are brought into use: spirit, soul, and psyche.

A text on spiritual alchemy should draw a distinction between its use of the terms spirit, soul, and psyche. There are no strict definitions of these, as their usages have lengthy and varying histories. The understanding given here is based in a highly fluid and illuminative, alchemical perception of existence, that functions through the wheel of the *opus*.

'Spirit,' which derives through the Greek *pneuma*, originally meaning 'wind' and 'air,' refers mainly to expression and atmosphere, the light of the ethereal body and its spectre. It is also related to 'ghost' and the German *Geist*.

'Soul,' which normally translates the Latin *anima*, refers to the seat of things, so to speak, the structure or entity itself that is understood here as the ethereal body and its vessel. It does not derive from the Greek. Aristotle used the term *psychê* in a similar sense, where earlier philosophers such as Empedocles would refer to the *daimôn*.

'Psyche' refers to internal activity, or conscious and unconscious activity, perception, reflection, etc. Originally, the Greek *psychê* was conceived in terms of lifeblood and breath, that which is alive in the body, that which animates. It later acquired various meanings, beginning with the Greeks. It is, essentially, the place of apprehension and perception; the 'eye' and reflective, mercurial mirror of the soul, the perspectival eye or spherical mirror; imagery one will see often in alchemical texts, sometimes with wings. It moves, shifts, descends, ascends, and transcends.

Its activities, the ways in which it acts and animates, involve the mystery of the Will; which will be discussed as the alchemical or occult Will. And then, of course, spirit, soul, and psyche merge; a formation occuring in terms of light and the mercurial essence of the subtle body.

The daemon then is, in a sense, all of these; spirit, soul, and psyche—but on the unconscious, invisible, or unknown level. Martin Heidegger, who did extensive interpretation of early Greek language, translates *daimôn* by the German *Ungeheuer*, the 'enormous.' It is the sublime side of beings, and of our being, that is without place in the natural, physical world, and, as such, it is larger than life; a kind of haunting form or anima, something that looms in things. It is the uncanny and the extraordinary that is within the ordinary, and is not the ordinary. Hence the ethereal body and its vessel may be understood as the human daemon. In a certain sense then, the daemon emerges and becomes a part of conscious life through an alchemical occultism.

The daemon was also, for the Greeks, descriptive of spirits in general, spirits of nature, genii and the like, who were lesser than the gods. This involves a type of animism of nature. A person's own daemon was also sometimes personified as a spirit, similar to Socrates' daemon. Christianity then adopted the conception as the 'demon' as an essentially evil designation, this having some basis in the Greek idea of the maleficent daemon. This is also likely to have occurred because the daemon was often related to the Underworld, which was transformed by Christianity into a wholly 'evil' and objectionable realm.

The ancient Greeks also depicted a *daimonion* eye. The daemon is related to a Cyclopean self by the Rosicrucian philosopher Manly P. Hall, as the Cyclops is "a monster of the astral light, the shadowy giant who abides amidst the shadows of mans own being."[8]

The ethereal body is also called the 'body of light,' and the solar body. The mercurial essence of this Other may be conceived as made of liquid light. This light is the body's aethers, or ethers, sometimes called ectoplasm, that belong to the complex and coloured structure of the body and its vessel.

For Hall the "natal daemon" is also "the diamond soul." This body is also called the diamond body and the rainbow body. The diamond represents an indestructibility, and it reflects the colours of the rainbow. And the diamond represents the *lapis*, the 'treasure hard to attain.' It is also the 'pearl of great price,' and the toad's precious stone.

Within the *opus magnum* the practitioner realises the subtle body through dreaming practices, as it is the body of light that dreams. And the physical body is then a type of dream the daemon creates, one might say. It is a congealing of light created by the subtle body, which is, in fact, more real than the physical body. And the acquisition of the stone involves a re-casting of the shadow through an Illumination. It then means the purification and regeneration of the daemon, and of the body and vessel as a whole. These are compared in alchemy to the purity of the dove, the unicorn, the white rose, or the lily, and to the extraordinary, regenerative abilities of the lizard or the salamander, and to the supernatural phoenix.

The Vessel

The alchemical vessel, or *vas hermeticum*, originated with the dawn of alchemy. It is the Vessel of Hermes, as named by one of the earliest known alchemists, Maria the Prophetess. It represents the human soul, its internal workings and aural field, and the egg-like envelopment of the body within that field.

Manly P. Hall describes this egg-like aural field within Kabbalistic theory:

> In the secret teachings of the Qabbalah it is taught that man's body is enveloped in an ovoid of bubble-like iridescence, which is called the Auric Egg. This is the causal sphere of man.[9]

It is the "AIN SOPH sphere of the entity called man." This sphere has varying understandings through Kabbalistic history. Scholem references the "brilliant shell," or *kelippath nogah*, the dark and 'evil' shell of the Other Side, filled by the light of the *Sephiroth*.[10] This shell then belongs to a counter-world, also a Luciferian world.

Hall also notes that it was nearly universal to pagan philosophies, called the opalescent globe, or soul envelope. It may have been known by the Greeks, as it was known by Galen.[11] And we derive its name in relation to the Greek goddess Aura. The idea of the vessel-egg as soul then extends into Christianity, and Christian art, as the aureola, and was brought into Christian adaptations of alchemy. And today we have theories of the human aural field understood in terms of energy, light, and colour, that have basis in early modern occultism.[12]

The alchemical vessel then, as this representation of the human soul, holds within it alchemical metamorphosis; from the Greek *morphê*, as change in an inherent nature that forms through its own light. The vessel-egg of the alchemical transformations maintains itself throughout the history of alchemy, developing at times into sophisticated apparatus, sometimes involving a crucible, or a retort for distillation. The transformation then, within this apparatus, involved alterations of substances, sometimes including metals, and accomplished through a firing. Through spiritual alchemy it may be metaphorically represented as the traditional glass oval, which becomes blackened, alighted, and then restored, or 'hermetically sealed,' through a purification.

The egg shape, as the encasement of the soul, is perceived in the most literal sense of a surrounding, hard shell. The aural field is often imagined as an aura that merely emanates from the body, but this is not its full nature. The aural field also possesses a shell-like encasement surrounding and encompassing the body and its light. The vessel, metaphorised as the eggshell, represents an actual encasement composed of layers of solidified energy that encompass the human body. Its layers are also a kind of spectrum. It erodes and decays during a person's life, and this coincides with aspects of the physical body's decay. Its shape fluctuates somewhat and bends slightly with the spinal column; though it is always only understandable in terms of a space and time that is infinite, and a field that has variable or infinite levels.

Israel Regardie describes the aural egg in his comprehensive work on the Philosopher's Stone:

> The egg of the philosophers refers to the aura, the ovoid emanation exuding from and surrounding the astro-mental form. It is this shape which is the subject of the work. When brought to fulfilment, it glows and scintillates most brilliantly like some more than precious gem.[13]

This light and gem then belongs to the *lapis* as it alights the vessel. The *lapis* is, in fact, the vessel's internal alighting, associated with its mercurial quintessence. Jung notes this in connection with the Holy Grail: "As the Grail is the life-giving vessel itself, so the stone is the *elixir vitæ*."[14] The Stone is the "light that conquers every light."[15]

The vessel is the occultist's essential area of activity. The term 'occult' means that which is hidden, concealed, or secret, as the vessel is the hidden side of a person's being. To bring about the alighting of the vessel is then a central goal of the alchemical process. This alighting is then utilised to purify the vessel, to balance it and make it whole. This light is also, through Hindu thought, sometimes called the 'core star.' It only becomes the *lapis*, however, when it is fully alighted. And this alighting is the Attainment of the Lesser Stone.

The Stone is then the internal alighting of the vessel:

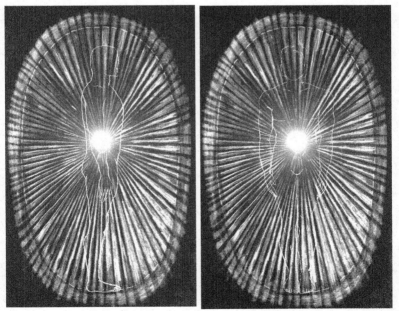

As the vessel is egg-shaped, it is represented by the bird's egg. And the transformations taking place are then understood as the birth or emergence of various significant birds. The metaphoric image of the soul as bird is an important aspect of the *opus*, belonging to its spiritual alchemy. The bird, in the forms of a variety of species, and its egg, will manifest in dreams once the alchemical process has been initiated. Each bird signifies the state of the soul, and the state of the vessel as a whole.

The Breath

Knowledge of the intimate relation breathing has with the alchemy of the body is ancient. This is particularly the case in Eastern alchemy and its history, as is well known. Chinese internal alchemy involves breathing techniques, as essential to focus on the internal life force, and on *ch'i*, psychic energy. Breathing is generally understood then to be utilised in practice, often combined with meditation, to purify the body and to collect and store or circulate energy. There are various traditional Chinese disciplines centred within, or associated with, internal alchemy, which are mainly Taoist disciplines.

This effect of the breath on the body's energy is often understood physically through the blood, and the relation of breathing to the blood, though there are other levels and powers of the breath to consider. Some believe the breath to be magical; and understandably so, because it does have transcendental affects within the body. The concern here, however, differs somewhat from traditional views, since the emphasis will be on the breath's ability to cause subtle vibration. The alighting of the vessel, located at the centre of the body and vessel, is subtly vibrated through the breath, and this enhances its ability to have effects on energy.

Castaneda provided two important, and perhaps original, methods of breathing. He prescribes the act of fanning the head while breathing, which enacts a type of cross motion that moves or cuts through energy across the entire body, and vessel, and its surroundings. And, he prescribes the act of returning in memory to the past events of one's life while doing this breathing, in order to dissipate ethereal effects from one's past.

The act of remembering past events is then simultaneously combined with this breathing, enacting a purification of the body and vessel, that extends through the entirety of one's past. Of course, returning in memory to past events as an act of healing has parallels in Western thought, particularly through psychoanalytic methods of healing trauma. With Castaneda however, this act is an entirely energetic and ethereal movement and activity of effects.

This breathing then, largely influenced by Castaneda's techniques, combined with the alighting of the vessel, is the means by which the vessel is purified. On initial or beginning levels this is experienced lightly and subtly, and on fully manifest and advanced levels it becomes a process of profound expulsions, of masses of undesirable energy. These masses are often very large and extensive, and are felt by the body, in the most literal sense, as substances, ranging from light, vaporous energy to very solid and heavy, almost metallic energy. Most of these substances will be energy from other persons, but they also include that of foreign substances, chemicals, and radiation, in short toxicants, and also disease; as everything that enters the vessel has an ethereal aspect, that is its centre or true force.

This more advanced level of breathing and purification is then described in detail in the subsequent work, *The Peacock's Egg*. It is visualised through an anatomy of the body and vessel, that is purified as an essential phase of the occult *opus*. And this purification is, in turn, a rebuilding, a replenishing and fortification, as one's energy within the vessel is one's own energy, which will naturally return and repair itself through this purification.

Visionary Alchemy

The early alchemists were visionaries, and their knowledge came to them through dreams and visions. Occultists are often enchanted by descriptions of visionary experience recorded by early mystics and others. And academics are often baffled by them. In ancient times visionary experience was more common than it is today. Life itself was more dreamlike, in some way, as dreams in earlier times were not distinguished from reality as clearly as they are today. Speaking on the level of the human body and psyche, this state of being existed because the psychical apparatus actually differed. The psychical apparatus is not a fixed entity, but is something which has abilities and mutabilities unknown to us. A change occurred over time which, one may say, occurred because of evolution of this apparatus. It might then be asked whether this limiting could be an evolution. But, within evolution aspects come forward and fall back and are not simply augmentive and cumulative. Our perceptual apparatus is now, in some ways, stronger than it was in ancient times, as is our conceptual apparatus. And then the earlier visionary, or less limited, aspects of perception can return in more empowered or comprehensive ways.

The experience of *dreaming*, as Castaneda italicises the word to draw a distinction, is a type of lucid dreaming. It may be differentiated from what has been called lucid dreaming by its emphasis on the assertion of an objective reality. He is referenced partly for this reason, as this assertion of objectivity not only enhances the visionary states of the alchemical *opus*, but this kind of *dreaming* also has an effect within the body and psyche, instilling changes within the psychical apparatus. A method of initiating *dreaming* practice is then outlined here in the following chapter, *The Opus Magnum*.

Dreaming enhances and augments the *opus magnum*. It causes the fullness of the alchemical path and its imagery to become clearly manifest, visually through the psyche. Every state, change, and movement appears as the practitioner undergoes the *opus*.

Alchemical dreams that pertain directly to the *opus* are often unusually bright and vivid. They often occur in an uncanny and instantaneous way. There is obviously something extraordinary about the way in which this happens, and no one knows how or why this occurs. The reason for their appearance seems to be that they are direct manifestations of one's own chemical vessel and its internal light and liquid light. At times they appear as static images, but usually there is movement and interaction between beings, often alchemical animals. And every aspect of the vision has some meaning or message. Once the *opus magnum* begins to take hold and move through its cycle these should occur at least once a week, sometimes daily, or nightly, and at times more than once in any single episode.

Alchemical imagery was not determined by any particular person, and also not by any group of alchemists, or by any history of arguments and agreements. This imagery is naturally formulated by the human psyche in itself. There are two important truths to know about this imagery: the human psyche, body, and vessel manifest their states of being through this imagery, and these states may be conveyed through a scenario or series of images, as change or movement.

The alchemical dream represents the full structural life of the states and movements of the daemon, and of the vessel as a whole. It manifests structural aspects of ourselves, through imagery, as personification, or as some representation, as the psychical archetype. Consequently, there may be a complexity to the imagery that represents that entirety. Hence the alchemical dream may contain a complexity or scenario-like nature depicting the psyche's full life.

The common dream is often a manifestation

occurring through a chemical reaction within the psyche or vessel, or through a deficit or lack caused by reactivity; which are not necessarily felt or experienced consciously. A chemical or an energy from other people, often accumulated through one's life, causes dream imagery to appear, which has little value other than to signal a chemical reaction or lack. And then, through the alchemical process, an active intentionality manifests, and a fullness, that transcends or supersedes this reactivity. Sigmund Freud's understandings of dreams can then be placed within this area of reaction, but is not an important issue here. The alchemical dream bypasses imagery, which Freud saw in dreams, that simply reflect subjective and personal needs and wishes, or transformed or disguised wishes.

There are then three types of alchemical dreams: The essential or typical alchemical dream, the visionary alchemical dream, and the low or rudimentary level alchemical dream. There is no clear line to draw between these, and they will merge with each other, but a distinction is made nevertheless.

The essential or typical alchemical dream is a distinct experience of a meaningful scenario or series of images that manifest clearly, and pertain, in some way, to the alchemical process. Having these dreams means that the psyche has definitely entered the pathways of alchemy. And the practitioner will certainly know these dreams when they are experienced; they have a bright, distinct, and uncanny quality, and a liquid clarity beyond that of the common dream. They often have a distinct message-like nature, at times, for example, in a one-two-three series of images or events.

The visionary dream is an experience similar to the essential alchemical dream but which extends beyond it through time, elaboration, realness of bodily experience, and interactions with beings or archetypes.

The low or rudimentary alchemical dream is usually simply a manifestation of one's own energy and alchemical structure as single image, often without symbolic meaning. These become significant for the recognition of substances within the body and vessel.

There are three other types of dreams that may occur, and at times merge with the alchemical dream. These other types are not an issue here but they will result and come about through the alchemical process. These are the so-called out-of-body experience,[16] the experience of being in other worlds, and what may be called the magical dream.

Again, lines of distinction are difficult to draw. The out-of-body experience will result from the alchemical process. A space and time between sleep and waking will open, in which visions will occur within the real space where one sleeps. And a result of this will be experiences of being in spirit form within that real space.

Another likely result of the attainment of *dreaming* will be the experience of being in other worlds for extended lengths of time. It is a truly strange and uncanny experience, not addressed here in full, but about which there is much to say. The practitioner will know when this happens, as the surrounding world will seem tangible and have all of the qualities of a real world. But this will obviously not be our world.

The magical dream or vision seems to cause something to happen or change that extends beyond the dream. It enters into a certain level of power that is beyond mere meaning or message. These can also involve spirits, angels, demons, and elemental beings, who may be indistinguishable in appearance and behaviour from real beings, and can even be conversational. And how real and authentic these beings are believed to be is, of course, up to the practitioner to decide. These appearances can contain real structure and energy which can be sensed and felt by the practitioner. They can actually have a psychological effect on the practitioner's energy,. And then some of these dream images may be mere illusions, and a distinction made between the real and the simple illusion may be difficult to make.

Dreams which pertain directly to the alchemical

opus and its phases, which is our main concern here, require explanation and focus. These generally do not contain force and life in themselves, so to speak, as they are brought about through the practitioner's own psyche. They are reflections of what occurs with and within the vessel, and may be seen as a looking into a metaphorical or symbolical soul, or daemon-mirror. This will be rich in imagery as the *opus* cycles through its paths.

An alchemical dream interpretation method is then given. This dream interpretation is not centred within a history of meanings, or within an eccentric or personal vision. It is based on the understanding that the vessel is manifesting through imagery. The vessel and all of its aspects, movements, positions, and states of being manifest in alchemical dreams. And this is essentially the definition of the alchemical dream. There is much similarity to Jung's dream interpretation, but differs, being centred on the idea of the human psyche and its energy and structure as an alchemical vessel.

In these ways a general interpretation of the alchemical dream will always be possible, though the specific and certain interpretation will often be left open to the practitioner. And those specifics will differ for each individual. What is emphasized then is not specific dream interpretation, but instead a basis or structure utilisable for the art of dream interpretation.

Every detail of the alchemical dream has meaning. It is not essential to know every meaning of alchemical dreams as they occur, to proceed through the circular *opus*, but this path is followed more closely if these are grasped. They can illuminate the practitioner's understanding of its paths and levels, so that one knows what is happening.

When combined with the alchemical process *dreaming* opens onto a kind of theatre, within its own world, or worlds, that has its own rules and realities. It is difficult to know then what is important or real there, and what is not real, and what 'real' aptly means. But, generally speaking, the alchemical dream is real because one's own soul-vessel and structure are real.

The Vessel

The vessel itself will manifest in dreams in two ways; either as some form of encasement or vessel, or archetypally as a woman.

The vessel may appear as a vase or bottle, or as any type of containment such as a box, a room, or a vehicle such as a car or ship. Or, as an egg. Its appearance as a simple object is sometimes a low, rudimentary appearance, where it conveys a simple image, while its appearance as something more elaborate can have deeper alchemical meaning.

The vessel then also manifests and is personified as a woman, as the vessel itself is a feminine entity. Jung associated this woman with the anima, and through Greek myth she may be associated with Ariadne. She can be of various natures, often mysterious, or maternal, though sometimes difficult to discern in dream imagery, obviously, because of the multivarious appearances of women. And then she appears transcendentally as the alchemical bride, and as the queen, which has further meaning. She is also, through mysticism, associated with the Kabbalistic *Shekhinah*, a feminine form of the verb *shakhan*, meaning 'to dwell.'

It is likely that her appearance will differ for the male and female practitioner. That difference is not specifically known here, but which may not be found in the imagery itself, as the vessel itself remains a feminine entity. Rather, it may appear through the character of the imagery, and the position of the practitioner in relation to that imagery. And, she has a male counterpart, manifesting through the king, and through the resurrection, death and rebirth, and renewal archetypes.

Birds

There is a traditional set of birds that will appear, and not vary, it seems, unless perhaps there is some difference related to cultural or regional backgrounds. These are the hen, raven, peacock, dove, and eagle or phoenix. These will appear based on the stage of the *opu*s one is at or within, or traversing, so to speak. This set is not limited, however, and will include other types of birds.

Another traditional bird likely to appear is the pelican. It represents the wounded state of the vessel within the putrefaction, as the pelican feeds it young with its own blood; and for many alchemists it represents a self-sacrificial aspect of the *opus*. The white swan is also traditional, with similar meaning as the dove; they both represent, at least on one level of meaning, a purity.

Generally speaking, the hen represents the beginning of the *opus*, the raven, or crow, represent the blackening of the putrefaction, the dove and white swan represent the purification, the peacock represents the many-coloured phase, while the eagle and phoenix represent the final phase of the *opus*.

There will be other birds that appear, such as the owl, the hummingbird, or the seagull. They will vary for meaningful reasons. For example, while the peacock will symbolise the peacock stage of the *opus*, and ethereal light as it is coloured within the vessel, the representation of colourful energy may appear as a parrot, perhaps relating coloured energy to the spoken word, or as a colourful eagle-owl if the energy is related to the eagle stage of the *opus*. There are no strict categories as the *opus* flows alchemically through its paths, and these birds can be surprisingly foreign to one's own knowledge and memory.

On the one hand they represent attainments, and on the other hand they do not. They represent phases of the *opus* as states of the vessel and soul, that will appear, disappear, and reappear variously.

And then the actions of the bird, as with all of the alchemical animals, will have significance. So, for example, a hummingbird taking nectar from a flower may refer to the soul acquiring energy through the circular *opus*, or something of this nature.

Serpent and Dragon

The serpent has a mercurial nature; it moves and shifts like pure liquid mercury. It transforms through the *opus* from snake to dragon, and also takes on a circularity, actually depicted in circular forms.

In many instances the serpent will appear simply as a snake. But, it also appears as a legged creature; the lizard, salamander, alligator, tortoise, and as the dragon. Both the salamander and dragon represent a magical or extraordinary state. Anything reptilian, it seems, will represent the serpent. It can even manifest as the dinosaur, its name being derived from the Greek *deinos* 'terrible' or 'potent,' and *saura*, 'lizard,' as the potent mercurial psyche, though perhaps in a certain primordial sense. And the tortoise may appear representing the serpent as the shell-vessel itself.

The serpent may be seen generally to signify the mercurial energy, and is often named as the Spirit of Mercury. One will notice when reading alchemical texts that a wide range of alchemical imagery are intended to represent Mercury. This is because most alchemical imagery represents some aspect or state of the mercurial quintessence. But, the serpent is the most essential representation of it. The serpent is the light of the psyche as pathos, perhaps related to the Greek Python. It is *Python*, *Phthon*, and *Phythonis in infinitum*.[17] It represents energy which is in a state of movement, vibration, and expenditure, and the energy which dreams and creates perception, and reflection. It is the pathos and manifestation of all of psychical experience and light of world and of nature, which then becomes the Ouroboros.

The serpent is then, in some sense, the path one takes and traverses—as what one has experienced and will experience; and as Mercury is also the god of paths. And then it is the various paths and pathos of the psychical energy itself.[18]

The Dragon is then a formation of the serpent,

and is an important manifestation in dreams. It indicates the presence of, and the encounter with, the supernatural, and with nature itself as extraordinary, or magical. The practitioner's position and level within the supernatural are shown by the appearance and behaviour of the dragon. It is the serpent combined with the eagle and the lion. It represents nature itself, and the world, as it traverses land, air, and sea, and nature as light itself, as the practitioner's full apprehension of light appears as the dragon. The Greek *drakôn* is thought to derive from *drakein*, meaning 'to see clearly,' and *derkonai*, meaning to see or look, as a flash or gleam. It refers to that which sees or looks, or that which shimmers or reflects, or to all of these aspects or apprehensions of light.

The Sanctuary

Often depicted as a garden in alchemical texts, the hermetic garden, often a rose garden, the sanctuary is the transcendental place or site of the practitioner's vision. In it the alchemical transformation occurs in its fullness of symbol and meaning. It is the place of the philosophical tree, or of the Sephiroth tree, and the mercurial fountain. Any of the alchemical images can appear there. It can be the Garden of Eden, or the Garden of the Hesperides. The enclosed garden, the *hortus conclusus*, is also, through Christian symbolism, associated with the Virgin. The sanctuary can also appear as a public square or arena, or manifest as a building of some transcendental kind, as a religious sanctuary, or as the citadel. The sanctuary is again parallel to the vessel, but represented through a living transcendentalism.

The Chymical Wedding should occur within the sanctuary. The groom, or daemon-body, will join with the vessel-bride, as the consummation of a fullness and wholeness. And the king and queen may appear within the sanctuary.

King and Queen

Alchemical manuscripts from early times depict a King and Queen. They perform various acts, often a marriage or coupling; which has its origins in the ancient idea of the 'sacred marriage.' And, strangely enough, they do also manifest in dreams, and will do so for the contemporary practitioner. The King is associated with the Sun, or Sol, and the Queen with the Moon, or Luna, and consequently with gold and silver. Their full meanings are difficult to discover, however, though they may be understood through the light of the vessel.

The King represents the alchemical light as mastery, dominion, and light of realm, of the *opus* as a whole. He is the Sun as manifestation, justice, and the light of day, and its gold, as he signifies that which has been attained and brought to light as fully present within the *opus*.

The Queen is the vessel itself and its mercurial silver. She reflects the light of day, as the Moon reflects the light of the Sun, and represents the hidden light of the alchemical process.

In some alchemical manuscripts the initial conjunction, or *coniunctio*, or coupling, of King and Queen, or merging of Sun and Moon, has a dark, sinister, a left-handed nature, and is even tragically Oedipal. In fact, the alchemists sometimes identified with Oedipus, as Oedipus Chymicus. Jung finds this sinister nature in the *Rosarium philosophorum*, where the king and queen are depicted with a left-handed handshake. This is essential to the transformative process, and signifies the eclipse, the dark conjunction, aligned with the blackening of the vessel.

The King and Queen also appear separately, and will sometimes do things that would not necessarily be associated with royalty. And their nature will manifest in various ways. The King's nature, for example, is present in the appearance of the Sun, or of the lion; though these also have separate meanings, existing within differing levels or contexts. Similarly with the Queen; her nature is present in the appearance of the Moon, and in any manifestation of the vessel, and the garden or sanctuary, and the bridal chamber.

To bring the *lapis* to the king is the completion of the *opus*, notes Jung. A dream may occur, for example, in which the practitioner brings crystals or diamonds to a king, or some similar dream, signifying that the stone has been brought into one's own mastery.

The Queen, being related to the sanctuary, will appear often within an enclosed area, such as the garden. She is the high, transcendental representation of the *vas hermeticum*.

The King and Queen then reunite, or in any case there is a second conjunction of King and Queen, as the Chymical Wedding, which represents the consummation and the wholeness achieved through the *opus*.

The Shadow

The putrefaction is a blackening, a *melanosis*. It is most often depicted by the crow or raven. It is often a poisoned and decayed state, also symbolised by a black serpent, or the black toad, and other dark images such as the Black Sun, or a black swamp, as that from which the stone emerges.

The putrefaction involves the Shadow, which is in essence the practitioner's shadow, as it permeates the light of the vessel.[19]

The Shadow appears in dreams in many forms. The Shadow will appear bodily, simply as a shadow-self. The self as person appears often in dreams as something separate from one's own perceptual standpoint. And often it is this shadow-self, which can acquire many guises. It can appear in an obvious way as a shadow or silhouette, or as other archetypal images, such as the monkey-man.

The shadow projects itself within alchemical dreams in various ways. At times it appears simply as a negation of something; for example, the black unicorn may manifest, or the toad may appear in the shadow of an elevated stone. Darkness and shadow permeate many aspects and images of the alchemical process, and these will manifest in dreams as such.

The shadow is not, however, simply a negative image or something undesirable. It is essential to the psyche and its light. It is transformed through the *opus*, becoming the occult shadow; which will be discussed further. The occult shadow is the Other self, the appearing non-appearance, so to speak, of the ethereal body that also becomes a physical body in *dreaming*. This occultation appears in its most significant, original state as a death moment, in which the ethereal body detaches from the physical body while in a semi-awake state. When this state has been entered by the practitioner the body has entered a spiritualised state in which it has taken a permanent step into its alchemical death.

Circle, Step, and Path

Often the structure of the *opus* itself, and its phases, will appear. This can occur in the form of a circle, such as a wheel, or in the form of steps or stairs. The circle appears as a flower, often a rose. The circle is also the metaphysical and surreal timepiece that measures the days of one's path.

The path of the psyche within the *opus* will appear simply as a pathway or street. And the steps will appear as stairs, or as a ladder. Often the specific number of steps will be significant, and indicate the phase of the *opus* referenced within the dream.

These may also combine with other meanings. For example, one may dream of waiting for a train, and its number is 271. The train represents the beginning of the journey of a cycle of the *opus*, and seven represents its phases, while one represents its final wholeness. The two may either indicate the second cycle of the *opus*, or perhaps the duality of King and Queen, or both.

The cycle and path can also then manifest in dark or shadowed forms. Examples of this would be the appearance of the spider or the octopus, whose eight legs refer to the phases of the alchemical wheel. The spider can also signify other things of course, and it is also the Black Sun, and Medusa's head. But these all refer back to the hindrance, poisoning, and constriction of the free-flowing nature of the alchemist's *opus*.

Another vision which may appear is the squaring of the circle, which may be depicted in various forms. It is thought to signify a separation into the four elements by some, though its meaning has various interpretations. The squaring of the circle is often understood as a method of producing the *lapis*, as the circle is squared and re-circled through a transformation.

Death and Rebirth

The alchemical death and rebirth are essential to the
opus, and this will be represented in imagery by a deity
or personal archetype. Most cultures have this
archetype in their history, usually being a male figure.
He may be the Greek Dionysos, the Celtic Cernunnos,
the Green Man, or the Egyptian Osiris. They are the
resurrection deities, figures of death and rebirth, or
figures of renewal.[20]

This rebirth will also be represented through the alchemical animals; for example, the serpent, who sheds its skin, and also transforms, or the mythical phoenix who arises from its own ashes and is reborn.

Two alchemical animals who closely represent the renewal archetype are the Stag and the Unicorn. In the *Book of Lambspring* these represent soul (stag) and spirit (unicorn). Their meaning is far-reaching and mysterious, however. They certainly refer to high attainment, and may be upheld through a strength and nobility of soul, and a supernatural nature of spirit. They are also symbols of masculinity and virility. And their manifestation belongs to the dawning of purity and Will. The stag is a symbol of renewal through its antler regeneration. The unicorn certainly signifies the extraordinary or magical.

Both the stag and unicorn have also been thought to signify Christ, who is, of course, another resurrection deity. Jung: "The stag is an allegory of Christ because legend attributes to it the capacity for self-renewal." And for the same reason "Mercurius is allegorised as the stag."[21] And the unicorn has a long history as representative of Christ.

It may be that the practitioner undergoing the *opus* will experience Christian imagery, even regardless of their own conscious beliefs or feelings. This was an essential part of Jung's visionary experience, who thought that the earlier resurrection deities foreshadowed Christ. This does not mean, simply, that religious imagery may occur, because the Christ image does not seem to come about simply because of religion. The reasons for this manifestation are unknown or uncertain, but this appearance involves the essence and essential movement of the *opus*, wherein the archetypes of Mercury and Dionysos are inherent in the Christ image. There is an extensive history of noting parallels between Christ and Dionysos. He is the Mercury that represents the mercurial quintessence, the aether-blood, related to the Dionysian death and rebirth and Dionysian wine.[22] And then the Passion is paralleled with the cycle of the *opus,* including the putrefaction, as its *tenebrae,* and the journey to the Underworld, as the *descensus ad infernos.* He is also associated with a number of alchemical animals, inclusive of the lion, stag, unicorn, peacock, pelican, dove, and the serpent. And then the Chymical Wedding is paralleled to the marriage of Christ and Sophia, or the *Shekhinah.* It is archetypal imagery that may be a kind of layer or gloss set within the whole *opus*, as the *opus* may become an *Imitatio Christi*, as the shadow is relinquished, so to speak, through the *Christ-Mysterium.*

And then the *rebis* will appear. It is an hermaphroditic being both male and female, as often depicted in alchemical texts, or may change from male to female or visa versa. The *rebis* represents the conjunction that has taken place, as the Latin *rebis* means 'double matter.' It is the dualism through which the rebirth occurs, sometimes depicted as a winged being. The *rebis* may appear at any stage, and its form may vary. The birds that appear are also sometimes thought of as hermaphroditic fowl.

The *magnum opus* then involves the reborn and renewed soul or daemon, which coincides with the aurora of the work, and the *lapis*.[23]

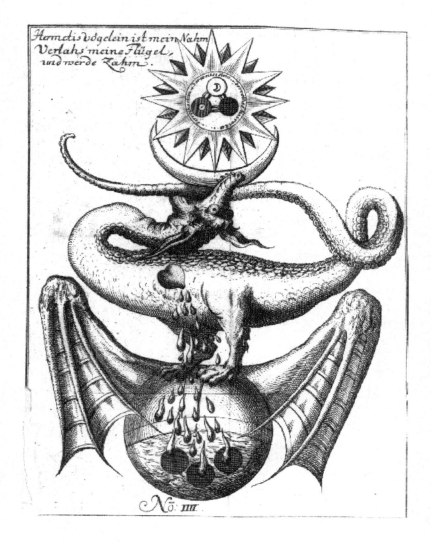

Aurora

Dawning as manifestation, the final phase of the cycling *opus*, will appear as imagery, in various ways.

The alighting of the vessel may appear as crystal formations, perhaps quartz crystals. And the diamond indicates an advanced final phase. In fact, crystal forms may appear representing the Lesser Stone, while the precious gem will represent the Greater Stone.[24]

As the final aurora approaches, the colour red should become an issue in dreams, in particular a scarlet, as well as bright yellow and sunlight. This is the time of manifestation, of evolvement, renewal, and luminosity of the day. The red lion sometimes represents this phase. It can be said in general that while the king is master of the realm, the lion is impulse or willing impulse and fiery force, and the sun is its manifestation. Hence, the dawn of the *opus* is always a brightening, as the rising sun. It is the turning, golden rose, and it is the springtime of the *opus*, and may also appear as the sunflower.

The amphibious salamander is also likely to appear at the later phase of the aurora, as may the Phoenix, the sun bird. And the Chymical Wedding also belongs to the aurora, as does the child, or golden child, representing the *lapis*.

The aurora may also be anticipated in some form. For example, the salamander may appear, underwater, in a vessel, eating a sunflower seed. Or, the Chymical Wedding may be anticipated, by a dream of the woman of the vessel involving a gold, diamond engagement ring.

There are other important alchemical dream images: the mercurial hare, the honey bee, the philosophical tree and tree branch, the apple, the dog, the wolf, the fish, the rat, tower, mountain, lake, moth, housefly, and some others.

An interest in interpretation of alchemical dreams might also lead one to consult Jung's voluminous works; though, in terms of dream analysis, he may not have been correct on every point. Jung, on occasion, can be too centred in psychoanalytic rhetoric for the occultist; for example, the serpent represents for him the 'unconscious,' whilst within more authentic alchemy it is seen to represent all of nature and its mercurial essences.

The practitioner should understand that since these images represent the structural and ethereal life of the psyche and soul, there may not always be a simple idea that will explain their meaning; similar to the way art is difficult to describe at times. These images manifest from a level that is not necessarily accessible through words, in a simple, categorical way, as alchemical images are generally not symbols or ideas exactly. They are metaphors on a level very close to the workings of the light of the soul itself. The description and understanding of the imagery should remain close to the level of the mercurial energy and its formations and movements.

An example of this mystery is the dog. The dog manifests often in alchemical dreams, and there may seem to be a simple explanation, but there is not, it is mysterious. It can be friendly or unfriendly. It seems to represent judgement in some way, a Cerberus of some breed, though it also seems to represent a part of one's state of being. Perhaps it represents the body's visceral state of being. And it has a relation to the domesticity of the house, as the house-vessel.

Transcendental colours will also appear, as already mentioned, and are usually associated with particular phases of the *opus*. Black, white, red, and yellow are the most significant, and the rose may also appear as these colours. There are traditional images emphasised with these transcendental colours; the White Queen or the Red King, for example. Another image often referenced is the Green Lion, wherein green represents the addition of mercurial sulphur to the *opus*.

What is important to know is that the alchemical dream signifies states, movements, and changes within the soul-vessel. And that the procession and success of the *opus* is taking place when important images appear.

The low or rudimentary level of the vessel will also manifest itself in images. Energy itself, the energy or light within the vessel, appears on occasion, and this is particularly the case when a pronounced affect is taking place there. And it will often appear as a specific colour. Colours of the vessel's aethers, and their various casts and consistencies, form the image of the Peacock's Egg. They are the vibrational pathos of the psyche, and of the psyche of others that have entered one's vessel. In terms of what enters the vessel, they will be either this human ectoplasmic energy, or the energy of foreign chemicals, or radiation sensed within the body.

Most often this will appear simply as a substance of some kind, of some weight or texture, which manifests through a simple reaction within the psyche. And this can appear within any dream, including the common dream, sometimes as a simple form, or often as something natural and active, for example as a body of water, or, typically, as a wild animal. It may also appear as a substance within a vessel of some kind, such as a drinking glass.

For the most part these images are not important, but the practitioner should know about them, and they will make more sense once the purification is fully entered. Their appearances can also be somewhat random, in the sense that something that is always changing may be viewed at a random moment.

The wild animal that represents this rudimentary level will have nothing embellished or elaborate about itself or its behaviour, appearing only through its image and movements. Its colour and texture may be related to the energy itself, for example a rhinoceros may signify hardened grey energy moving within the vessel. It may also merge with the appearance of the alchemical animal, though the true alchemical animal will be of a natural or a transcendental colour, that is not related to this lower level. Jung notes something similar, wherein wild animals "indicate latent affects" in dreams. But he combines this with alchemical symbolism, so that a lion, for example, indicates "the danger of being swallowed by the unconscious" in alchemical terms of a "fiery" nature.[25] As a rule, one might say, if the animal is somehow embellished or presents some meaningful context then there is something more than a lower, rudimentary level occurring within the image, as it enters the archetypal alchemical realm.

Another type of low level alchemical image that will appear, caused by energy movements, is a type of still, shadowy image, usually of a person or body part, that indicates damage done to the ethereal body. They are shadowy as they appear like simulacra, distorted or exaggerated images, often caricatures. They are instantaneous images that indicate changes taking place at their moment of appearing.

Ordinary dreams can often be low level dreams in this sense, as they may involve something that is taking place within the vessel on a rudimentary level. Perhaps on its most rudimentary level it can even involve food being digested; with the understanding that there is, nevertheless, an ethereal level taking place. But, these elementary images become significant in terms of one's health. Aspects of one's physical health will appear on this level, which is a separate area of knowledge, beyond the alchemical dream. And how they may be utilised is a separate matter from the alchemical process. It is worth noting, however, that physical health is sometimes indicated for mysterious reasons by the appearance and behaviour of a house-cat. And healing can be indicated by the appearance and actions of the toad, as the toad's body also represents the vessel that transforms poisons.[26]

Herbal and medicinal alchemy have their own history and branches of knowledge. Herbal alchemy may be said to belong essentially to internal alchemy, since its main focus is medicinal; though, it also has external applications, such as making incense. It crosses over into dreaming practice through herbs that are thought to increase or enhance lucid dreaming, and through other means such as sleeping pillows.

Another area of herbal alchemy is that of the hallucinogen, as already mentioned in connection with the psychoactive toad, and which includes the toadstool. The main point to be made is that hallucinogens are essentially something that concerns the awake visionary experience, while the alchemical vision will occur during sleep or during half-sleep, wherein hallucinogens need not apply. The full *magnum opus* will be accompanied by visions that do not require chemical assistance, as they will occur naturally during sleep.

It might be asked, however, if hallucinogenic drugs should be included in general alchemical practice, or in occult practice. Again, this question pertains to the visionary nature the psyche may attain from an awake position. There are, obviously, pros and cons, and, of course, the inclusion of hallucinogens is another issue left to the discretion of the practitioner. Apart from obvious reasons why they should be avoided, of dangers, bodily damage, and illegalities, they can also give a false sense of attainment; because whatever is accomplished through them is generally not repeatable without their use. And the practitioner needs to stand on their own on their occult path. On the other hand, certain hallucinogenic drugs can loosen the psyche in a person who may have difficulty, and can also cause profound experience in the practitioner. It is best to consider that the purpose is not to damage perception, making it vulnerable or flimsy, as damage can give the illusion of visionary ability, but rather to develop perception through strength and expansion. One might ask oneself if hallucinogens will be of benefit in practice, and if one has the physical and mental strength to handle them or not. The advice is then to follow texts on the subject as drugs are used in occult practice, as there are these texts, and not to simply follow the modes of the recreational user.

Some general words of advice are given, regarding a person's focused involvement with dreams and visions:

The practitioner may find it necessary to be cautious not to allow *dreaming* and visions to become *confused* with reality. One should maintain reality as reality, and dreams as dreams, with the new opening of a third space of dream-reality. Some persons are able to easily maintain a strong grip on the real, everyday world, and others may not be.

Because of the realness of *dreaming* experience an issue of false memories can arise. On occasion one may have to reckon with oneself to discern whether an experience took place in dreams or in reality. But, there will always be an aspect of the *dreaming* experience that will be impossible in reality.

When that is recognised the experience can readily be distinguished.

In the case of alchemical dreams, another issue may arise, the practitioner may begin to notice, of images and events that seem to be related to the alchemical dream, manifesting in life, either prior-to or following the dream itself. This enters another mysterious area of dream analysis. It involves deciphering coincidence and synchronicity, and the idea of the precursory image, sometimes a dark precursory image, and the after-image or after-effect. While the practitioner may become aware of this as an issue, what becomes undeniable, and also startling, is that it is the alchemical dream that is the centre and ground, regardless of what occurs first in sequential time. True alchemical dreams are never simply transformations of prior images or impressions, though they may seem to be on occasion. And in terms of alchemical dreams this synchronicity will not occur often enough to become an issue.

The Opus Magnum

The *Opus Magnum* is completed through cycles, that include steps or phases. The cycle is separated into a number of phases through which the *prima materia* is transformed into the Stone, wherein the stone emerges and manifests through its own light.

The three essential phases, historically speaking, are a blackening or *nigredo* that is the putrefaction, followed by a whitening or *albedo* that is a purification, and then a reddening or *rubido* that coincides with the dawning of the *lapis*. Often there is also a yellowing, or *citrinitas,* that is a solar light and sometimes coincides with the *rubido*. And then within these phases the Peacock's Tail, or *cauda pavonis*, the many-coloured phase appears.

Often there is a conjunction, called the *coniunctio*, symbolised by the *coitus*, of King and Queen, or as the merging of Sun and Moon, and therefore as the eclipse that blackens. It is an essential aspect of the putrefaction, and is also a merging of the shadow with the practitioner's psyche. These then separate, so to speak, and there is a further unification at the cycle's dawn, as the Chymical Wedding.[27]

The alchemical process then involves three cycles, while the stone as internal alchemy is understood to have two distinct manifestations through the second and third cycles: The first being the attainment of *dreaming*, the second being the alighting of the vessel, and the third being the manifestation of the occult Will. These cycles together complete the *lapis philosophorum*. The second cycle may also be understood as the attainment of the Lesser Stone, while the third cycle attains the Greater Stone.

The cycles are illustrated within an occult circle.

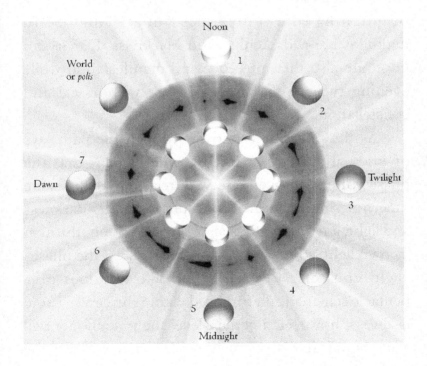

The circle is often utilised in occult practices. Its cyclical movement and encompassing scope may be implemented to attain or manifest any psychical intentions. The circle and its coinciding pentacle natures have been understood as practical in attaining the will, or what one wills, as was understood by Éliphaz Lévi.[28]

The occult circle also has a history of many forms of segmentation. Because of the metaphoric representation of the moment, and the emphasis on perception, image, and experience of light, they are related to times of the day. Dawn and noon are a brightening and appearing while twilight and midnight are a darkening and blackness. Dawn and noon are also then presence and manifestation while evening twilight and midnight are withdrawal and constellation.

As the practitioner moves through the pathways of internal alchemy it will become evident that the phases of this process are very real, but at the same time not simply linear. Every phase has its darkness and light, and midnight is also a type of noon, through its own light, so that this wheel will spiral as the phases alight and refer to each other, like the lines of a pentacle schematically imposed within the circle. There is always, however, a certain level the practitioner will stand upon at any given time, and that will also be evident through the manifestation of imagery.

The light of these phases is then also the alchemical mercury, the quintessence as it constellates and gathers, as its *logos*,[29] that formulates, dawns, and appears. Jung notes this relation of the alchemical light to astronomical metaphor:

> The peculiar expression *astrum* (star) is an alchemistic term that approximately means quintessence.[30]

Hence the astral body, the *corpus astrale*, is the quintessential body that constellates its formations through the alighted phases of the *opus* that manifest at its dawn.

The sun then metaphorises the visionionary world and its light, including the power of that light and its source. It is the King and his light of realm and mastery, Helios and his light of radiance and revelation, Apollo and his light of dream and measure. The alchemical solarity is also a type of illuminative solitude, called the *solificatio*. It is the practitioner's manifestation of the Sun-Will, appearing on the psyche's horizon.

The practitioner's methods then aim to achieve three specific changes within the body, and the *opus magnum* is separated into three cycles pertaining to these: the Attainment of *Dreaming*, the Attainment of the Alighting, and the Attainment of the Will. These cycles are the basis of the full alchemical process the body undergoes and accomplishes its transformations through. Most of the alchemical imagery will appear in both the second and third cycles, though in differing forms in each. The attainment of *dreaming* and the attainment of the alighting are emphasised here, while the more advanced cycles, the attainment of the alighting and the attainment of the occult will, are re-examined and emphasised in the subsequent work, *The Peacock's Egg*.

The Attainment of Dreaming

Noon
The ordinary dream occurs. The decision is made to augment the opus through the power of vision, and to evolve the vision.

Putrefaction
The ordinary dream is seen to be formed by the human shadow.

Twilight
The dream as it is dominated and controlled by past effects is set aside and relinquished.

Purification
The psyche is cleared of thoughts and concerns, and preconceptions.

Midnight
The blackness is entered wherein the quintessence of the ethereal body is apprehended.

Formation
The intention is set.

Dawn
Dreaming occurs of itself. The initial act of the occult Will as it emerges.

A method of exercising *dreaming* is given. There are many methods that have been offered to exercise dream control and lucid dreaming. And this is a basic method that will work when enacted with patience and effort.

The initiation of *dreaming* practices requires an intention set within oneself, which should be set well and unyielding, on a deep level. This is an act of intention that will take time to manifest in dreams, perhaps many months. But, the manifestation will occur as an uncanny surprise in dreams, so uncanny that it may not be recognised appropriately after waking. Suddenly, a dream will become strangely real, as if some outside force has imposed the same sensorial realness and depth of reality one experiences in life into an unknown scene. The surroundings seem to acquire real structure and their own momentum. It will prolong itself independently for some length of time, in the same way that our world does, though for a limited duration. And once this has occurred, in a full sense, a number of times, it will then occur on its own without prior conscious effort. In this way a threshold is attained.

Meditation in this sense of initiating lucid dreaming is a withdrawal from thoughts and everyday concerns. It is not an ecstatic or emotional state, or prolonged meditation. And it is not a withdrawal from the senses. It is a simple, singular moment in which a direction is given to the self and body; which can be accomplished by an image, or an imaginal act that depicts what one intends.

This is initiated by an act of Will. It is the beginning of the experience of an occult Will. The practitioner isolates the psyche and performs a commanding intention. This is accomplished through a meditation, a state of blackness, and a silence, in which one simply excludes everything from the psyche other than an intention. There are no interfering matters in the mind or in feelings, as if nothing else matters.

Dreaming is also accomplished through intentional enhancement of the perceptual apparatus, by creating a kind of dream-aware psyche. Viewing one's daily world for lengths of time as if in a dream, as if looking at an unknown or foreign scene, or image, can be advantageous, rather than simply taking things as already-known. For some length of time one apprehends the world as if being in a dream-world, including full, side-to-side scenic vision, with full attention to the scene. This can also be done while walking. It should not be done while operating a vehicle, obviously, because there is a loss of central focus, though it can be done effectively as a passenger.

The practitioner also acquires the ability to raise consciousness within dreams. When *dreaming* occurs the practitioner acknowledges that this is taking place, and then proceeds with intention and balanced control. According to Castaneda this may include an awareness of the body by looking at one's hands.[31] This device is helpful and important, but can also accomplish little with time, as the real matter is internal to the practitioner's psyche and body.

The practitioner then holds the *dreaming* for as long as possible. This requires a certain severity and power that may be acquired through experience. It is a natural act the practitioner will sense, and is often best accomplished through activity that is not too sedentary and not too active, such as walking. But one also holds doggedly to the dream, with the psyche and with the whole body.

Dreaming readies the body for its own alighted and perceptual evolvement, and becomes a strong part of the practitioner's life and nature. *Dreaming* can also be frightening and horrific at times, which the practitioner will quickly discover. But, it enhances the visionary nature of the *opus* and it awakens the central *lapis* within the body, as this centre is also the place through which the dream is perceived by the body. By the time this second nature has become set well in the body and soul, and the psyche has been suffused with perceptual experience that is not of our common world, the path toward the Lesser Stone will already be underway.

The Attainment of the Alighting or The Lesser Stone

Noon *The time of the initial vision and light. Dreaming has been accomplished.*

Putrefaction *The vessel is open as the cast shadow permeates its interior. The eclipsed or blackened sun illuminates the opus.*

Twilight *The day's illusion is relinquished, and the vessel or structure is revealed and experienced.*

Purification *The purification of the vessel is undertaken without the full alighting.*

Midnight *The blackness is entered wherein the quintessence of the peacock's egg is apprehended.*

Formation *Formation of structure and body.*

Dawn *Initial alighting. Access to the aethers is attained.*

The appearance of the noonday sun, which is a metaphor for the visionary state of the practitioner's psyche, is now beyond that of the common psyche. The practitioner has acquired a visionary psyche that is dreamlike, clear, and fluid.

The vessel is now in a state in which the shadow may be cast upon it and may permeate it, involving the practitioner's intention to transcend the shadow, and recast the shadow.

Though this darkness exists within the vessel, the evening twilight reveals the truth of this darkness. As the dream-illusion is relinquished at noon, the truth of the darkened vessel is revealed, in its structure.

The occult shadow appears at evening twilight. It is the *daimonion* shadow-body and its vessel, though still tainted by the human shadow through the putrefaction. Twilight then is the complex in-between time of the practitioner, its limbo, when the vessel has appeared in its full structure and begins to manifest, but is still impure and attached to the world of the day's human shadow.

Through the night and the midnight of the *opus* the daemon seeks to emerge and become fully manifest. The alighting of the Stone and the Stone's power to purify the vessel are initiated. To purify the vessel, and its surrounding field, essentially means to empty it of all energy except what is one's own; a process through which one's own energy also replenishes and rebuilds itself naturally, on its own. All energy within the vessel that is not one's own becomes accessible for expulsion through the alighting, with the exception of natural nourishment and the like. And a lengthy purification praxis is begun.

Another exception to this emptying of the vessel exists in the form of a special amber energy. It is something like honey, and combined with an outer white glow of the vessel and an inner silvery metallicism, it gives the whole egg a golden appearance. It is a naturally shared energy, also discussed in-depth in *The Peacock's Egg*.

The peacock's tail then appears within the vessel. This metaphorises the many colours of the aethers within the soul, and may be called the Peacock's Egg, appearing in its splendour. The vessel and its body are now established as light and structure that will be gradually purified, strengthened, and rebuilt.

This renewal of the vessel begins at its dawn, which is the alighting of the Lesser Stone. The human shadow is gradually cast off, or recast, through this alighting and its force and act of purification. The alchemical dream then presents this process to the practitioner as it occurs and the psyche traverses its path.

The alighting may occur in degrees or subtle stages, and whatever degree of alighting occurs is always permanent. It is also a hidden and unfelt experience that will only be noticed through its abilities to effect energy. When it occurs in its first truly manifest state, within the second cycle of the *opus*, its beams are clearly felt, because they contact resistances within and surrounding the body. They are something like bendable poles that alight in whole extending areas, based on a natural intentionality.

The alighting in itself, of the *lapis* centre within the body and vessel, is an imperceptible light. This occurs in instantaneous degrees of brightening, which will also symbolically manifest in dreams. The dissipation of undesirable energy is caused in part by the brightness of the *lapis*; which is why that dissipation becomes more expedient, massive, and fluid as the *opus* progresses. In its highest state the alighting is like a flame that requires only an intentionality to burn and dissipate undesirable energy within and surrounding the vessel. The brightness of the *lapis* centre is also not entirely constant, as whatever degree of brightness it has attained is permanent but also occurs through an intentionality. What occurs through the *opus* is simply a change in the limit of the alighting, a light which exists in all people. And, in fact, this may be said regarding the *magnum opus* in general—that it is an expansion of limitations.

When the alighting fully manifests the body is no longer human. This will not be fully sensed or self-evident until the purification is accomplished, which can take many years; though, this change is also gradual. But it is, nevertheless, the case that the body is no longer a human body as, among other things, there is a permanent change in the ways in which affects are experienced. And then perception is also evolved, as a change occurs within the psyche itself. And the daemon becomes too dark and too bright for human perception, and no longer lives under the human sun.

The Attainment of the Will or The Greater Stone

Noon
Dreaming acquires the images of the alchemical process.

Putrefaction
The shadow takes an occult form, and the black sun is dissolved.

Twilight
The alighted structure is fully attained and made central.

Purification
The purification is completed. The vessel is sealed.

Midnight
The blackness that reveals the pure quintessence of the dove's egg, from which emerges the eagle or phoenix.

Formation
Constellation, gathering, and logos.

Dawn
Final Illumination and Will.

Once the alighting has been attained *dreaming* will have acquired an alchemical nature, and through the purification the practitioner will be on the pathway to the Occult Will. The pathway is then fairly certain, however the purification may take many years, depending on the person and their history. This is due to the massive quantities of energy that accumulate in the vessel. The specific methods of the purification are described then in *The Peacock's Egg*.

The *opus magnum* involves a rebirth. A spiritual death-moment occurs within this rebirth. The spirit and psyche will detach from the physical body within a real space in the world, most likely during sleep, within the space where one is sleeping. This occurs in a highly resolute, physical manner. In this way the body is spiritualised and one can say that the occult shadow has fully manifested.

Through this spiritualisation and alighting the practitioner will purify the vessel and realise this aural field and its structure as occult truth and reality. In this way the psyche re-centres itself within this structure, as it transits from its old centres within the ego, mind, feelings, etc. Or, in any case, the psyche is recentred from its place within reactivities occurring within the vessel, and their feelings, sometimes mistaken for the 'soul,' onto a place of the vessel's own light and structure. An appropriate statement is made by Heidegger regarding this kind of re-centring of the psyche:

Becoming free means binding oneself to what is

genuinely illuminating, to what makes-free and lets-through, 'the light.' [32]

As the human shadow necessitates and fixes the human world, through reactivity within the vessel, that pervades the psyche's life, that human perceptual world and its limits are relinquished. And so, the alchemical purification becomes a true perceptual evolvement.

A new blackening takes place. It is a new darkness that results from the purification, a true blackness that precedes and brings dawn to the alchemical Will. It is a black abyss, a natural midnight and void, that is also replete and fecund through the new power of the vessel.

The occult Will may then manifest. It already had existence, as it exists in every person, and is also the force behind the initiation of *dreaming*. It can symbolically manifest in alchemical dreams. The lion has this significance as the impulse or instinct, though it can more distinctly manifest, for example as a dagger or athame. And the dragon is, perhaps, its most profound manifestation of force and reflection.

The occult Will is not simply something to do with having or doing what one wills. It means that a natural wholeness has been attained wherein the fullness of one's own energy is intact and available to the psyche. Speaking on the level of the vessel's energy itself, purity is more or less equivalent to power and quantity of energy. Purification of the vessel means that one's own energy returns to its natural place within the vessel giving it its full power and potency.

The *opus* then acquires a circular depth wherein a midnight act of constellation and the gathering of psychical image, of force and Will, precedes a dawning or aurora of manifestation. It is dawning which can be simply growth and flourishing, or that of light and illumination, or the worldly formation of dream and vision.

It is, in its highest state, the attainment of the pure or extraordinary gold, the 'philosophical gold.' It is the resurrected golden body, of the *aqua aurea*, the golden, mercurial energy. It is also the *aurea apprehensio*, the golden apprehension or awareness. It is then a *eudaimonia*, a joyful, true happiness of the soul and of the daemon. It is also perhaps related to what is called *Xian* in Taoist alchemy, and perhaps the *Sahu Ka* of ancient Egyptian alchemy.

A new occult shadow is cast. In fact, therein lies the secret that enacts the occultist's Will, and changes or alters his or her own self and dream, through displacing or altering the shadow; as the shadow is the differentiator between the ground and its perspective and the sun and its light of day, and the body. And as the shadow is more real than the illusionism of the body, the occult shadow, however well grounded, becomes the psyche's bottomless abyss.

Practical Apparatus

Including within praxis the vessel as a physical apparatus, a vase or receptacle, of whatever kind, is always an option. The usefulness of involving an actual alchemical vessel in practice depends on the individual practitioner. It is certainly not necessary, and it can be included at any point in time. Some prefer a ritualistic occultism while others prefer simply the internal and meditative. A classic example of this difference may be found contrasting the occultism of Aleister Crowley and that of Austin Osman Spare, and his criticism of Crowley's ceremonial magic. There are advantages to the inclusion of the actual vessel, however.

The physical vessel allows the practitioner to involve a certain level of activity in practice, and may be an addition to the occult paraphernalia they are accustomed to. In essence it represents the self, the occult self or soul, or daemon. The fact that it is simply there in presence is the main issue, because it can involve itself with the practitioner's dreams and visions—something like a scrying glass. There are many fine apothecary jars and other vessels available for this purpose. And this visionary manifestation occurs regardless, as it will be the case that a vessel of some kind will appear in dreams, or in visions occurring within the space where one sleeps or resides, that indicates something through imagery. It will not only indicate phases of the *opus*, but will reveal other things, such as the state of the practitioner's body.

The vessel has parallel forms in occult and religious histories, including the Holy Grail, the genie's lamp, and the witch's cauldron. Ideally it will be a glass ovoid. Obviously, this is appropriate because one can see into it then, but Jung notes another reason for the glass:

> Transparent glass is something like solidified water or air, both of which are synonyms for spirit.[33]

It is the *aqua permanens*, and the Ariadne vessel of light formed of the 'bright and clear fluid of Bacchus.'

Of course, the alchemists did much with their various vessels, as they were transforming actual materials and substances, often firing clay or luted vessels, and attempting to transmute metals. In terms of spiritual alchemy the alchemist's fire coincides with the 'burning love' of the mystics. And the practitioner may perceive this fire as the intentional and deep internal fire that alights their pathway.

Jung comments on the practitioner's artifice:

> The bottle is an artificial human product and thus signifies the intellectual purposefulness and

artificiality of the procedure, whose obvious aim is to isolate the spirit from the surrounding medium.

Jung is noting that the practical vessel, or artificial vessel, represents the 'intellectual purposefulness,' or the practitioner's spiritual intentions. It exists on a level that signifies the practitioner's intentionality, mirroring his or her own spirit-vessel. The spirit within the vessel, which is the essence of the work, is isolated, or given a type of presence, by the vessel itself. It is then a device allowing the Will and art of the Artifex to objectify itself to some extent or degree. And then its artificiality gives it a distinct level of its own, something similar to the way in which religious objects are perceived. It is a sublime object that is no longer an object.

In a certain sense the question of whether to involve the practical vessel within occult practice has to do simply with the fact and question of the occult 'object.' Generally speaking, occult objects in practice are devices utilised to direct, move, or transform energy, or in some way to wield or manifest energy. The practical vessel then belongs to this area.

The vessel is then implemented by bringing it into the circular process of the *opus*. The manner in which this is accomplished depends upon one's specific practice to some extent. But, its presence alone is the essential issue, because the visionary manifestation of the vessel is then given an intended setting and place.

Straying slightly from the topic—One of the acts of *dreaming* is to enforce an objectivity into dreams. An advanced level of *dreaming* is acquired when the practitioner can hold an object in hand within dreams, for some length of time. It will be indistinguishable in its realness from objects in reality. The practitioner acquires a serene and detached relation to the objects that appear and are acquired within practice.

For some implementation of the actual vessel can be an advantage, for others it may not be, and can also be a distraction from their own internal centring and attention. Its device will not decide, ultimately, on the success of the internal alchemy of the *opus,* as that will be determined within the self. But, another practical addition to the *opus*, which is highly advisable, is the book.

The occultist's book, of whatever kind, may be used to record progress through the *opus.* The vessel may also be illustrated there, of course. But, the book may be used to record alchemical dreams, and most importantly, when the peacock's egg is realised, to record energy changes. This will keep a record of energy expulsions that have and have not been performed.

Here the vessel is depicted containing the alchemical *homunculus*:

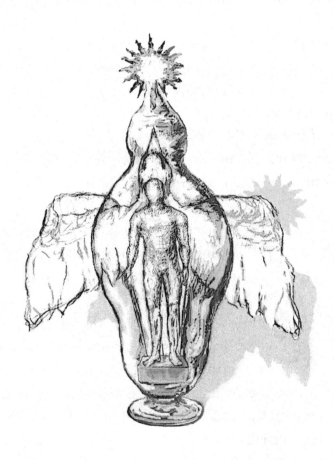

The Darkness
of the Day

*And when his Corps the force of vital breath began to
lack,*
*This dying Toad became forthwith like Coal for colour
Black:*
Thus drowned in his proper veins of poysoned flood;
For term of Eighty days and Four he rotting stood
By Tryal then this Venom to expel I did desire;
For which I did commit his Carkass to a gentle Fire.
  from *The Vision of Sir George Ripley*

The putrefaction is the phase of
blackening, sometimes called Saturnine
Night, or Night of Lead. It is involved
with the Journey to the Underworld, the
shadow kingdom of the dead, and is
viewed as a dangerous undertaking, a time
of testing and initiation. Achilles was
dipped into the river Styx in the Underworld to make
him invincible. And through the act of *dreaming* this
journey actually occurs. The practitioner's psyche,
along with its *dreaming* body, actually goes to the
Underworld as a part of the *opus magnum*.

To undergo the putrefaction means to enter the blackness of the Shadow. It means to enter one's own shadow, and to transform it, or to recast it, wherein this task is necessarily difficult in nature, and like a shadow, elusive and vague in its graspability. The overcoming of the human shadow cannot, it seems, be explained through any type of science, or at least this explanation has never been fully accomplished. There is, however, much to know about it.

This transfiguration does not mean that all shadow is dispelled and overcome. There is an evolving into a new light, and consequently a new shadow. The necessity of the shadow is noted by Nietzsche:

> . . . the shadow is as necessary as the light. They are not opponents—rather do they hold each other's hands like good friends; and when the light vanishes, the shadow glides after it.[34]

Within our circular *opus*, the cast shadow changes direction at the high noon of the putrefied black sun, and becomes the transformed occult or evening-twilight shadow. Entering this shadow is then the essence of an occultation, which is always already hidden in the human shadow, one might say. To enter the evening-twilight time of the occult sun, or invisible sun, to transfer oneself there, to that space and time, and its shadow world, is the essence of the occultation of the psyche. Evening twilight is the timeless-time of this occultation—. It is not the morning's dawn of illumination and light of life and world, and it is not the blackness of night and of constellation. It is an Other time, when the light of day falls away, and yet the hidden structure, of the shadow's invisible theatre, remains illuminated.

It may be called a time of the Invisible Sun, in alchemical terms. This twilight time, and other side

of the world, is illuminated in modern art by Giorgio de Chirico. He was also involved with occultism, and knew alchemy. And various other modern artists entered a visionary occultism, while much of modern art can be viewed from the standpoint of the shadow. But, the time of evening-twilight is a type of seeing, an apperception, one might say. It is also a type of metaphysics; which is not a metaphysics of the 'mind' and of ideas, but rather an occultation of the body and its psychical structure. It is a relinquishing and a disillusioning of the day's sun and light, that reveals the invisible sun, the light that casts the occult shadows, and the light of the true Dionysian metaphysics.

This relinquishing, disillusioning is also the solar dissolving and dissolution, enacted by the sulphuric-vitriolic Green Lion. It is then the impulsive laughter and indifference of the occultist's will to power; as it is described as the 'green and gold lion without cares,' in the *Rosarium philosophorum*. The practitioner is the sun dissolver, who reveals the true darkness of the day, and its serious, luminous alchymistry, prior to the sun's time of setting. And the regicide who reveals the secret king. The occultist is the bond-breaker, the disjoiner of the yoke or jointure that enforced the day's common truths, and common light and darkness. The Dionysian irrationalist who breaks the day's centre of light and reason in its time. The occultist is then the law-breaker, because he, or she, breaks the laws of physics, and enters the hidden twilight and its invisible, stark brightness, wherein the dream-world is possible, and reveals the hidden orderings of cosmos, of light and aether. To break and to reform are essential to the *opus*.

This occurs at noon because then all is laid bare, as the shadow disappears through its time of absolute vertical light. It is not the bare core of the dark abyss of midnight, but the bare reality of high noon when everything is revealed—and therefore nothing is revealed, because the bare truth of midday is as much an abyss as the black abyss of midnight.

The day's shadow, or the human shadow, can be viewed as the very essence of the unsolved, and unresolved, the solar incompleteness. It is the dark lack and distorted imperfection or incompleteness of the unfinished, the unfulfilled, the absence of *telos*. It is then also the thought, the thinking, that becomes silenced at the abyss of high noon, the time of the anticipated fulfillment of the *opus*.

What then is the Shadow itself? On the one hand, thinking in terms of light and shadow becomes obscure and ungraspable, and on the other hand it gets at the very heart of the matter. The essential idea to grasp is that it is the shadow that emits the unseen light of things, so to speak, the hidden truth behind illusion. We unveil the world and find the shadow world. And to know that world is to be an occultist. The shadow exists because the psyche in itself is light and reflective light, through its spherical mirror and internal landscapes. Without the shadow there is no form, and nothing can be real, as there would be only light. The most heavenly world casts shadows. This landscape is a type of realm wherein the alchemical imagery is formed and takes place, a kind of metaphysical theatre that exists under a light of its own sun. This realm is what the alchemical cycle seeks to change, through change in its spherical perspective.

This theatre is what is revealed in the alchemical dream, though it exists continuously whether or not it is seen. And the shadow is the necessitator of the realm. It is the call to repeat the same light and ground that it abides through. This act of holding down, of limitation, is ambiguously wanted and unwanted. And ultimately what takes place is a kind of *mastery*.

The King's shadow is the medicine man behind the king, notes Marie-Louise von Franz.[35] And while the king is master of the realm, he enters the blackening of the putrefaction; as depicted in many alchemical texts, as in fact, it is the king who is blackened. The king is blackened and undergoes a change, as he metaphorises the mastery of the *opus* and its sunlight of realm. Jung describes this blackening, eclipse of the sun, and its descent: "The king constantly needs the renewal that begins with a descent into his own darkness." And so, each cycle of the *opus* involves a renewal of the king, or sun, that re-alights the occultism of the king, as his shadow, as he is renewed through the undertakings of the *opus*.

The first cycle of the *opus magnum* overcomes the human shadow through the balance, intentionalities, abilities, or virtues, one might say, required for lucid and controlled dreaming. It is the human shadow and its weaknesses that impede dreaming and its manifestations, and cause its losses of lucidity, control, and realities. This overcoming of the shadow is a difficulty, but the most onerous phase of putrefaction occurs during the second cycle of the *opus*, wherein the shadow is most deeply altered. Therein, the alighting occurs, through a confrontation with the shadowy nature of one's deeper psychology.

This overcoming occurs through a similar approach to the shadow as that perceived by Jungian psychology; and so Jung's understanding is of value. There it is accomplished through a relation between patient and analyst, who brings about the patient's shadow through words and analysis. It is a disclosure and a disillusioning, but, this armchair approach may not suffice for the occultist who seeks the true Philosopher's Stone.

Since shadow is not something that simply

disappears, it then reappears, it changes or changes its position. This is part of the enjoyment of the *opus*, as it is a mastery of light. And since that mastery is already entered into by the practitioner through controlled dreaming practice, the shadow will manifest on its own, both in dreams and in life. In fact, this is the initiation of the alchemical *opus* and the blackening of the *prima materia*, or the human body.

The shadow may appear through common experience, that the occultist may not be inclined to avoid, in a common way, as a new occult path is opened. It can also manifest as provocation through another person or through other persons, who present real force and danger of defeat. Overcoming the shadow cannot be accomplished on one's own because the shadow is never what oneself may think it is, or like it to be. And if its overcoming is not somehow necessary, somehow forced, then it may win the game, so to speak, as its distorted light may then reign within the vessel.

M. Esther Harding, in her work on psychic energy and Jungian psychology, describes the experience of the shadow in life, as it limns a person's vulnerabilities and reactive points:

Reactions of this kind take place regardless of the individual's conscious attitude, and it often requires a high degree of discipline and inner development to hold one's ground in face of them. That intangible something called morale depends not a little on this ability. For experiences of this kind attack a man at the point where he is least protected. They can unseat his reason and make him act quite strangely; they can throw him into a panic or in extreme cases even into insanity.[36]

The human shadow delineates a person's points of entry, speaking in terms of the vessel, its weaknesses. These points are never precisely definable with words, but it is often through words that they are opened, like wounds; sometimes through truths, sometimes twisted truths, and sometimes through lies. The self-image is its hidden reflection, and pity and fear are its secret feelings. And so it necessarily becomes something highly elusive and vague.

While this reactivity takes place, the ethereal level of the vessel is being putrefied. And the point does not lie in allowing this to happen, though it always will, unless the practitioner is a truly gifted exception, but to surpass this reactivity, through an asceticism of a kind, or through "discipline and inner development" as Harding says. And how this surpassage is attained, and whether or not it is successful, is a great mystery, and also variously depends on the person. Of course, the alchemists understood the attainment of the stone in terms of divine bestowal. But, in any case, being set and well grounded on the alchemical path is an indication of one's abilities to realise the *lapis-aurora.*

One way to understand the shadow is as that which limits and delineates; it is that which makes real, in a certain sense, as artists know. And so to master the shadow is to master one's limits and delineations, which are pre-set, so to speak, by the human shadow.

The putrefaction has two qualities in general: Its dark nature and its poisonous nature.

Its dark nature involves the darkness of the shadow that is overcome or mastered. First as the human shadow that influences dreams. Then as the human shadow that corrupts the vessel, which is then purified. Then as the occult shadow that is mastered.

Its poisonous nature is mainly overcome through the second cycle, as there it most distinctly involves the impurity and corrupting of substances; aligned with the conjunction-eclipse. Chemically the *coniunctio* is the poisoned and putrefied state that results from the merging of the shadow with the vessel and its internal alchemy. It is based on affects, those affective chemicals, the invisible chymicals, that originate from the world, and from other persons, that are often so through the human shadow.

The shadow enters the soul, the vessel, to a point which demands overcoming. And the practitioner traverses the path of the *opus* further through this overcoming, and then by a purification. This merging with the shadow then becomes the reborn, the lightning from a dark cloud. While the blackening of the vessel demands overcoming and alighting, the alighting happens unexpectedly. Lightning signifies a "sudden, unexpected, and overpowering change of psychic condition," according to Jung. And he refers to the Chymical Wedding where "lightning causes the royal pair to come alive."[37]

The moon is associated with shadow, also called the 'toad's mirror' as the toad is sub-lunar pareidolia; it blocks the sun's light casting shadow on the earth. Its light is a false light, a pseudo-light, as it reflects and distorts the light of the sun, and outshines the stars and their powers of constellation. It is traditionally a symbol of deception and darkness, and also of dreams. Dreams belong to the pseudo-realms, which, through an occultism, become real. They become real through a hidden alighting, which occurs through the effort that alights the practitioner's dreams, and through the step to overcome the shadow that limits those dreams. The bringing of dreams into a sunlight of world is an act that continues through all three

cycles of the *opus*, as they will all enhance and empower dreams.

Despite its darkness it is wrong to understand the shadow in a moral way, just as it is wrong to understand light as such. Both the human shadow and the occult shadow can be related, in certain ways, to things that have historically been called 'evil.' Understanding the shadow in this way can lead the practitioner to mistakenly believe its forces may be overcome through a moral goodness, which can also be shadowy, and which will fail to suffice. Likewise, it is wrong to think the shadow may be overcome through suffering, though there may be suffering involved, as suffering, in itself, despite its serious nature, is pathos that cannot have effect there.

The following famous quotation from Shakespeare's *As You Like It* is appropriate by its imagery. But, it also contains a wise and enduring resolve in its surmounting of adversity; spoken by Duke Senior, exiled in the Forest of Arden, where he finds solace in nature.

Sweet are the uses of adversity,

Which, like the toad, ugly and venomous,

Wears yet a precious jewel in his head;

And this our life exempt from public haunt

Finds tongues in trees, books in the running brooks,

Sermons in stones, and good in every thing.

I would not change it.[38]

Free of the court's domain he affirms the darkness

of his existence through the forces and mystery of nature. Affirmation of existence and of the blackened sunlight of the world's day can let free the natural flow of the alchemical cycle, that may be impeded otherwise. It is the blackened sphere that is dissolved and separated, made distant, as a return to the natural truth held by light itself. In a certain way, the overcoming of the human shadow is itself a kind of naturalism.

In understanding the putrefaction, which is also signified by the raven, the coloured, ethereal world of the peacock enters the *opus*. The peacock's world is the place of the coloured affects that occur within the vessel—the pathos, persuasions, etc. of the ethereal affects of others and of the world in general. And the peacock's world can also be a dark world, of decay and vengeance, and of the essentially reactive spirit. It can be the place of more or less benign affects, and also comprises the soul's liquid, ethereal level of the repressed, sublimated, or transformed vengeance of the human shadow, which all persons have. The weightless shadow is the source of the heaviest weights, as the shadow creeps up, so to speak, on a person. The vessel then houses the level of the detrimental affects of adversity, and one's vulnerabilities, and therein lies its dangerous nature.

The peacock's appearance, however, traditionally indicates the success of the *opus*. And once the alighting is augmented, and the spectral aethers of the peacock's egg are fully accessed, the purification of the vessel is fairly certain, regardless of the state of things. This purified state may then manifest in a dream as the dove, long before the purification is completed; though it never will be entirely completed, as impurity is a natural aspect of being alive. The issue is to master the vessel to a point where it is unhindered and unencumbered, an act which also relinquishes the human shadow. The human shadow is left behind, like a detached, emaciated dead body; which may also appear in dreams.

The shadow is overcome through a distancing, the crossing of a bridge on one's path. It is a detachment, and a key to the success of the *opus* is that its initial intention does not originate from the human shadow, because it may then draw itself back into itself. And within the encounter with the shadow one comes to realise that it is not merely one's own shadow, but also an encounter with the limiting and oppression of the human world, and its poisons and fixations; which are very real. And so real opposition is not inappropriate, as there is an extent to which the alighting occurs through the overcoming of a resistance.

The shadow is both distortion and darkness, and therein lies its mystery, like the mystery of Dionysos. Its obscuration is the transgression and loss of the sun that are transition and change, as it enters the darkness that summons a new light of day, wherein its new reality appears.

Alchemy and Philosophy

Alchemy has a history within Classical and Western philosophy apart from Hermeticism; which is not always specifically stated or revealed within its texts. Many of the aspects of the alchemist's perception of the world, of matter and the elements have parallels within philosophy. The practitioner should know, for example, that the invisible, occult energy important to alchemy has a basis in the Pre-Socratic philosophers, and has also never been disproven or invalidated by any modern or contemporary science.

The alchemists were called Philosophers of the Fire. The unknown element essential to alchemy, often called 'fire,' and sometimes related to aether, is present throughout ancient Greek philosophy. The Pre-Socratic philosophers contemplated the existence of an invisible energy or substance, and an infinity belonging to its existence. Thales, Heraclitus, and Empedocles had these conceptions, including Anaximander's *apeiron*. Thales' assertion that all is water, and the great utterance attributed to Heraclitus, *panta rhei*, 'everything flows,' and the Heraclitian 'fire,' can be related to alchemical understandings. This extends on to Plato, who thought the four elements to be derived from a common source or *prima materia*, which he associated with the heavens, and with Chaos.

Spinoza, who studied alchemy, has a conception of an infinite substance. He and the Pre-Socratic philosophers were then an influence on Nietzsche, who is one of the most important thinkers for contemporary philosophy. And Nietzsche, in turn, has been a great influence on modern occultism, inclusive of Jung, Crowley, Spare, and many artists.

Nietzsche has a conception of the ether as primal matter.[39]He was fully aware of alchemy and its conceptions. Alchemy and the Philosopher's Stone are important for him; as these are revealed to be essential to his own *magnum opus, Thus Spoke Zarathustra*.

This philosophical context is not necessary to the success of the *opus*, of course, as it is, in many ways, a silent path, wherein even the language of words and conscious thought become secondary. Though, the daemon does its own kind of thinking; a kind of solitary, silent thinking. Something similar is described by Heidegger, as "the inner conversation of the soul with itself," which "proceeds altogether without sound."[40] But, Nietzsche is mentioned for those interested in contemporary philosophical and literary accompaniment to the *Opus*.

It is uncommon to hear alchemical understandings of Nietzsche, but in fact there is this important context to his philosophy. His work *Thus Spoke Zarathustra* is perhaps the greatest alchemical book ever composed, as it is a book of transformation written through alchemical imagination and metaphor. The resurrected body, or golden body, may be associated with his conception of the overman, and with regards to the shadow: Zarathustra says, "a shadow came to me—the stillest and lightest of all things once came to me. The beauty of the overman once came to me as a shadow."[41] The shadow is important in philosophy, just as light is, because, among other things, it refers to negation. But, Nietzsche places emphasis on its characteristics, knowing that the shadow has contemporary significance.

Both Jung and Heidegger wrote extensively on Nietzsche's *Thus Spoke Zarathustra*, as it is a mysterious work that has been variously interpreted. The issue here is to point out that Nietzsche perceives a metamorphosis of the psyche through alchemy, as it achieves a 'golden nature.' And that he has a conception of the Philosopher's Stone, which also brings about the peacock and its colours within the vessel. The Peacock's Egg is thought here to be essential to the vision Zarathustra describes in the section "The Vision and the Riddle" of this alchemical work of Nietzsche's.

He went back to the early Greek view of the world, revealing what was lost through changes that occurred in later times, in the same way that alchemy lost some of its original understandings. In turn Heidegger, who is often coupled with Nietzsche because of this semi-return to the archaic, also endeavours some reinterpretations of the early Greek. And, unbeknownst to him, perhaps, this offers insights into the *opus magnum*, bringing alchemy closer to that time, when it originated.

Often this simply means the occult experience is taken out of its centring in the mind and in ideas, and placed into the deeper or more unconscious levels, into dreams, silence, the viscera, and the abyssal un-ground of the soul, so to speak. This is also based in the 'inversion of Platonism' Nietzsche was interested in. Plato aligned his highest Idea, the Platonic Good, of the Platonic sun, with the heavens and with the *prima materia*. That light also seems to coincide with changes in the human psychical apparatus that occurred during that era. Nietzsche then does something similar, though in a much different, or opposite way. He brings a new definition of the Good, the *agathon*, or 'that which empowers,' into philosophy through, one might say, a new view of

THE BLACK TOAD ᪥ 121

the *prima materia*. And the religious alchemist, particularly the Christian, may also take an interest as he seems to think the influence of the Platonic Good within Christianity to be erroneous.

The common view of the physical world, though it is not really prevalent, developed through Natural philosophy, based on the natural sciences, and on classical mechanics, centred in Newtonian physics. (Newton was also an alchemist for a time, which exerted influence on his theories.) But, originally *physis* was experienced in a more dreamlike and luminous way. Heidegger understands the Heraclitian fire in terms of light and *physis*. He links the root of the word *physis* to *phaos* (light).[42] This has some basis in today's physics, mainly through Einstein; though generally not to the extent that may interest the occultist.

That earlier view has basis then in Nietzsche and Heidegger, which extends into the human psyche and the ways it is understood. The reader may notice that there is performed a de-emphasis of language and prejudices found often in spiritual and psychological literature; such as mind, consciousness, ego, or an unconscious, or libido; often referenced as the important forces and centres of things. These are replaced, so to speak, by the ethereal body as a whole, its light and vessel, a deep perspectivism, and an alchemical will.

The quest for the philosopher's stone is, in some ways, a search for something known by earlier mankind, which also has a place in contemporary philosophy.

Notes

1   [ ] Carl Gustav Jung, *Psychology and Alchemy, The Collected Works of C.G. Jung*, tr. R.F.C. Hull (London: Routledge & Kegan Paul, Trench, Trubner & Co., 1940-), 12, p. 321.

2   [ ] Ibid., p. 317.

3   [ ] Jacob Boehme, *Signatura Rerum, The Signature of All Things, and other writings by Jacob Boehme* (London: J. M. Dent & Sons, 1912), p. 89, §47. See also, for example, Antoine-Joseph Pernety, *Treatise on the Great Art: A System of Physics According to Hermetic Philosophy and Theory and Practice of the Magiserium* (Boston: Occult Publishing Company, 1989), p. 68. "The body is by itself a principle of death," as "it represents the shadows."

4   [ ] Johannes Helmond, *Alchemy Unveiled*, tr. Gerard Hanswille and Deborah Brumlich (Canada: Merker, 1991), p. 14.

5   [ ] C.G. Jung, *Alchemical Studies*, Collected Works, 13, §170, §190.

6   [ ] Gershom Scholem, *On the Mystical Shape of the Godhead: Basic Concepts in the Kabbalah*, tr. Joachim Neugroschel (New York: Schocken,

1991), p. 263. The terms *tsel*, *tselem*, and *tselamim*, 'images,' are connected through an etymology.

7   [ ] Boehme, *Signatura Rerum*, p. 89, §48. For an image of the two Mercuries see Michael Maier, *Atalanta Fugiens, The Flying Atalanta or Philosophical Emblems of the Secrets of Nature* (1618), Emblem 10.

8   [ ] Manly Palmer Hall, *Lectures on Ancient Philosophy: Companion to the Secret Teachings of All Ages* (Los Angeles: Penguin Putnam, 2006), pp. 289-92.

9   [ ] Manly Palmer Hall, *The Secret Teachings of All Ages: An Encyclopedic Outline of Masonic, Hermetic, Qabbalistic, and Rosicrucian Symbolical Philosophy* (San Francisco: H.S. Crocker, 1928), "Fundamentals of Qabbalistic Cosmogony," p. 117.

10 [ ] Scholem, *On the Mystical Shape of the Godhead*, p. 78.

11 [ ] Referring to the phrase *to periechon hemas*, or 'that which encompasses us'; a conception familiar to Galen of Pergamon, according to Scholem. (cf. Scholem, *On the Mystical Shape of the Godhead*, pp. 318-19n.)

12 [ ] The essential modern pioneers whose works cover the scope of the aural field and its energies include, Annie Besant, C. W. Leadbeater, Walter J. Kilner, Hippolyte Baraduc, William Walker

Atkinson, Auguste Marques, and Edwin D. Babbitt.

13 [ ] Israel Regardie, *The Philosopher's Stone: Spiritual Alchemy, Psychology, and Ritual Magic* (Woodbury, MN: Llewellyn, 2013), p. 24.

14 [ ] C. G. Jung & S. M. Dell, *The Integration of the Personality* (London: Routledge and Kegan Paul, 1940), p. 174.

15 [ ] Jung, *Psychology and Alchemy*, Collected Works, 12, p.76.

16 [ ] This is referenced as the 'so-called' out-of-body experience because the idea that something comes out of the physical body is based on certain prejudices. It might be more accurate to say, something splits off and reassembles itself, which may be called the daemon, and leaves behind it the simulacric illusion of the body.

17 [ ] Julius Gervasius of Schwarzburg (ed.), *R. Abrahami Eleazaris, Uraltes Chymisches Werk* 65 (Leipsig, 1760), Samullis Baruch, *Donum Dei* (Erfurt, 1735).

18 [ ] The reader may wonder about an etymological connection between the words 'path' and 'pathos.' To connect them etymologically it would have to be claimed that the Greek *patos*, meaning 'path' or 'way,' and *pathos* were related in meaning; where

'τ' is the voiceless dental version of the aspirated θ, similar to the way *agatos*, 'deserving admiration,' may be related to *agathos*, 'good' or 'that which empowers.' It is also questionable, however, that there exists an historical connection between the English 'path' and the Greek *patos*.

19 [ ] Jung understands the putrefaction as, among other things, a merging of the shadow with the 'ego.'

20 [ ] These associations are based on the likelihood of archetypal dream manifestation, and not necessarily on established historical facts regarding the death and rebirth archetype.

21 [ ] Jung, *The Structure and Dynamics of the Psyche*, Collected Works, 8, p 293n.

22 [ ] These associations have an extensive history. See, for example, the Bacchic and Mercurial imagery in Giovanni Bellini's *The Blood of the Redeemer*, 1460-65.

23 [ ] A curious thing happens within the rebirth of the second cycle of the *opus*. The practitioner then acquires an occult age and birthday. On occasion, somewhat yearly, at some time interval, which may be longer than a year, someone, or something, will wish the practitioner a Happy Birthday in an alchemical dream. It is a strange

occurrence that may at first be overlooked as normal dream psychology. But it is not; it is an authentic part of the practitioner's rebirth through the *opus*. It is not clear what the timing of this birthdate is, and it may be related to phases of the *opus*, as its dawn is always also a kind of rebirth. But it is a cumulative number, and if the practitioner asks within the dream his or her age the number will be stated.

24 [ ] Also see Jung, *Psychology and Alchemy*, Collected Works, 12, dream 24, on quartz crystals and the diamond.

25 [ ] Jung, *Psychology and Alchemy*, Collected Works, 12, p. 190.

26 [ ]Through abilities acquired as internal alchemy it follows that the practitioner may, if one so chooses, become an authentic healer of others, of some kind. The extent to which this is possible is not known or investigated here; though, the sound advice would be to first complete the cycles of the *opus* within oneself until a profound level of detached strength is accomplished, while healing abilities may also be augmented.

27 [ ] There are other more detailed phases often mentioned, though they refer mainly to the chemical operations of laboratory alchemy. There

is a calcination, which is the firing and heating of the vessel. There is often, following the conjunction, a separation, which may be seen as coinciding with the separation of the spirit or daemon from the physical body. There is a fermentation, which coincides with the putrefaction, and distillation, which coincides with the purification. And then there is a coagulation, which means the addition of salt to the fire, as the formation of the *opus* is made solid and real in its constellation.

There is also an elemental triad traditional within alchemical processes, of sulphur, mercury, and salt. Mercury is important to spiritual alchemy, where sulphur and salt, though they can be related to spiritual praxis in various ways, are not as emphasised. In general, sulphur is the green vitriolic and fiery agent that initiates change and transformation, and salt is the agent to formation and physicality.

28 [ ] Éliphaz Lévi, *The Magical Ritual of the Sanctum Regnum, interpreted by the Tarot Trumps*, translated from the Mss.of Éliphaz Lévi (London: George Redway, 1896), § V.

29 [ ] *Logos* is a Greek word with a history of interpretations. It is usually associated with words and language, and logic, though Heidegger notes

that originally the Greek *logos* stood in "no direct relation to language." (Martin Heidegger, *An Introduction to Metaphysics*, tr. Ralph Manheim (New Haven: Yale University Press, 1959), pp. 104-5.) It may be understood as the gathering and constellation of images in the psyche. And those images are not merely pictures in the mind, as the body itself and its world are images.

30 [ ] C. G. Jung & S. M. Dell, *The Integration of the Personality*, p. 222.

31 [ ] Carlos Castaneda, *Journey to Ixtlan* (New York: Washington Square, 1991), pp. 96-104.

32 [ ] Martin Heidegger, *The Essence of Truth*, tr. Ted Saddler (London: Continuum, 2002), §8.

33 [ ] Jung, *Alchemical Studies*, Collected Works, 13, §245.

34 [ ] Friedrich Nietzsche, *Human All -Too-Human: A Book For Free Spirits*, tr. Paul V. Cohn, Part II, *The Wanderer and his Shadow*, Preface, p. 173.

35 [ ] Marie-Louise Von Franz, *Shadow and Evil in Fairy Tales* (Boston & London: Shambhala, 1995).

36 [ ] M. Ester Harding, *Psychic Energy: Its Source and Its Transformation*, Bollingen Series X (Princeton: Princeton University Press, 1947), p. 314.

37 [ ] Jung, *The Archetypes and the Collective Unconscious*,

Collected Works, 9, part I, p. 295.

38　[　] William Shakespear, *As You Like It*, 2.1.12-18

39　[　] *"The world ether as primal matter."* Friedrich Nietzsche, *Unpublished Writings from the Period of Unfashionable Observations*, tr. Richard T. Gray (Stanford: Stanford University Press, 1995), 19[132], p. 44.

40　[　] Martin Heidegger, *Nietzsche*, volume 2, "Who is Nietzsche's Zarathustra?" He is referring to the Greek *dianoia*, 'to think.'

41　[　] Nietzsche quotes himself, *On the Genealogy of Morals & Ecce Homo*, tr. Walter Kaufmann (New York: Vintage, 1967), *Ecce Homo, Thus Spoke Zarathustra*, §8.

42　[　] "The radicals *phy* and *pha* name the same thing. *Phyein*, self-sufficient emergence, is *phainesthai*, to flare up, to show itself, to appear." (Heidegger, *An Introduction to Metaphysics*, p. 85.)

Index

CPSIA information can be obtained
at www.ICGtesting.com
Printed in the USA
LVOW13*2143010818
585694LV00017B/228/P